# RENOVATING A
# BATHROOM

**FROM THE EDITORS OF Fine Homebuilding**®

The Taunton Press

03-1848

## The Taunton Press
Inspiration for hands-on living™

The Taunton Press, Inc., 63 South Main Street, PO Box 5506, Newtown, CT 06470-5506
e-mail: tp@taunton.com

Distributed by Publishers Group West

DESIGN AND LAYOUT: Cathy Cassidy

COVER PHOTOGRAPHERS: Front cover: Roe A. Osborn, courtesy *Fine Homebuilding,* © The Taunton Press, Inc.; Back cover (left to right, top to bottom): Kevin Ireton, courtesy *Fine Homebuilding,* © The Taunton Press, Inc.; © Claudio Santini; Jefferson Kolle, courtesy *Fine Homebuilding,* © The Taunton Press, Inc.; © Christopher Irion.

Fine Homebuilding® is a trademark of The Taunton Press, Inc., registered in the U.S. Patent and Trademark Office

The following manufacturers/names appearing in *Renovating a Bathroom* are trademarks: Advanced Composting Toilet Systems®, Air-Loc®, Akemi®, Alkco®, American National Standards Institute®, Amerec®, American Standard®, Aqua Glass®, Axson® North America Inc., Barclay Products Ltd®, Basco®, BioLet®, Briggs® Industries, Brilliance®, Broan®, Chevy®, Chicago™, Climate Panel®, Clivus Multrum®, Coastal Industries®, Comet®, Custom Building Products®, Delta™, Diamond Tough Tools®, Doan's Pills®, Drano®, Duschqueen℠, Eljer®, Energizer®, Fluidmaster®, Flushmate®, General Electric (GE)®, Gerber®, Gold Seal®, Hans Grohe®, Hardibacker®, HEWI®, Impregnator®, Incinolet®, Jacuzzi®, Juno®, Kallista®, Kohler®, Lasco®, Laticrete® International Inc., LifeShine®, Luxury Bath Systems®, Maax®, Mansfield®, MAPEI®, Marley®, Miracle Sealants & Abrasives Company®, Moen®, Mr. Shower Door®, Mr. Steam®, Myson®, National Kitchen and Bath Association℠, Ninja Turtles®, NuTone®, Omnipanel®, Owens-Corning®, Phoenix®, Polyblend®, Prominence®, ProSoCo Inc.®, Qmark®, Quiet One®, The Radiant Panel ™ Association, Rensselaer Polytechnic Institute℠, Runtal®, Scotch-Brite®, ShowerToilet®, Slant-Fin®, Spanner®, Stadler-Viega™, Sterling®, StoneMasters ™, Sun-Mar®, TEC®, Teflon®, Tile Council of America℠, Toto®, Ultra Seal®, Vacuity®, Warmboard® Inc., Warmrails®, Waterworks™, Xenon®, and Zoë Washlet®.

LIBRARY OF CONGRESS CATALOGING-IN-PUBLICATION DATA:

Renovating a bathroom / the editors of Fine homebuilding.
        p.  cm. — (Taunton's for pros/by pros)
Includes index.
    ISBN 1-56158-584-X
  1. Bathrooms—Remodeling.  I. Taunton Press.  II. Fine homebuilding.
III. For pros, by pros.
  TH4816.3.B37  R45  2002
    643' .52—dc21                                   2002010192

Printed in United States of America
10 9 8 7 6 5 4 3 2 1

Special thanks to the authors, editors, art directors,

copy editors, and other staff members of *Fine Homebuilding*

who contributed to the development of the articles in this book.

# CONTENTS

Introduction     **3**

## PART 1: DESIGN

Ten Important Elements of a Good Bathroom     **4**

Accessible Bathrooms     **12**

A Gallery of Favorite Bath Details     **19**

## PART 2: SHOWERS, TOILETS, FAUCETS

Choosing a Toilet     **26**

How to Install a Toilet     **36**

Plastic Tub-Showers     **44**

Installing a Leakproof Shower Pan     **54**

A Walk Through Shower Doors     **62**

Residential Steam Showers     **72**

Choosing a Lavatory Faucet     **77**

## PART 3: TILING

Tiling a Bathroom Floor        **88**

Tiling a Tub Surround        **97**

Tiling a Shower with Marble        **106**

Tiling with Limestone        **113**

Silicone Caulking Basics        **123**

## PART 4: LIGHTING, HEATING, VENTILATION

A Look at Bathroom Lighting        **128**

Choosing and Installing a Bathroom-Vent Fan        **136**

What's Hot in Bathroom Heaters?        **142**

Credits        **152**

Index        **154**

# INTRODUCTION

**Y**ou might think that a builder's best work should be reserved for the living room, or maybe the kitchen, the big public parts of a home. But consider the bathroom. Where else do people sit for extended periods of time with nothing better to do than scrutinize the width of your grout joints or the state of the caulking around your bathtub?

But close scrutiny aside, there are other reasons why bathrooms demand a builder's best work. On a square-foot basis, bathrooms are the most expensive rooms in a house, in part because they aren't just lavatories anymore. They're also miniature health spas where we seek sanctuary from the stresses of modern life.

Bathrooms have come a long way from the outhouses and wash basins of our forbearers. But the price of all that comfort and convenience is tremendous complexity. They are intense little rooms, condensing electrical needs, plumbing fixtures, and ventilation into as little as 40 sq. ft. Fortunately, this book is here to help.

Collected here are 18 articles from *Fine Homebuilding* magazine. Written by architects, builders, plumbers, and tile setters, these articles will help you design a great bathroom, choose the right materials for it, and install them correctly. Unfortunately, the information in this book won't guarantee you'll have time to soak in the tub once you install it. But if you do, the grout joints will look beautiful.

—Kevin Ireton,
editor-in-chief, *Fine Homebuilding*

# Ten Important Elements of a Good Bathroom

■ BY DAVID EDRINGTON

I t's one of the first rooms we see in the morning and one of the last rooms we see at night. It's certainly among the most private rooms in the house, and the finishes, fixtures and mechanical equipment required by even a simple bathroom place it among the most expensive real estate in the house. Given the intimate nature of bathrooms and the frequency with which they are used, I think their design and detailing should also impart a measure of emotional well-being to their users. In this spirit, I offer 10 suggestions for making a good bathroom that can enhance some of your everyday experiences.

## 1. AN ENTRANCE TRANSITION

Except for the so-called master bath, most bathrooms serve several users and need to be placed in a location central to these users, usually halfway between the private parts of the house and the more public parts. Don't have a bathroom with multiple-door access.

Instead, create an entrance with a space outside the door—maybe an alcove off the hallway that gives some privacy from the main rooms or circulation area and has a little room inside the door before reaching the bathroom fixtures.

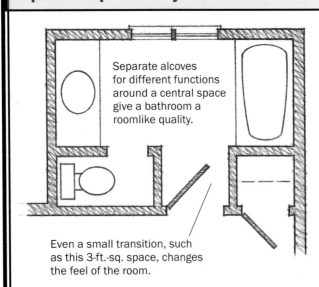

**An Entry Transition and a Central Space Improve Any Bathroom**

Separate alcoves for different functions around a central space give a bathroom a roomlike quality.

Even a small transition, such as this 3-ft.-sq. space, changes the feel of the room.

**Roomlike proportions add a calming touch to a bathroom.** A bathtub alcove such as this one creates a sense of place in a bathroom that just can't be achieved in a bath that resembles a hallway.

## 2. ROOMLIKE PROPORTIONS

Too many bathrooms are simply hallways with the fixtures lining one side of the hall. It is hard to make a pleasant room of that shape. First, a good room is roughly square or rectangular with length-to-width proportions not exceeding 2:1. In almost every good room, there is a clear central space, a center with smaller spaces like alcoves around the edges. A bathroom can be designed using these principles in miniature. There can easily be a central space that contains the entry, with some elbow room for washing and drying off and with alcoves around the edges for the toilet, the shower or the tub.

## 3. A GOOD WINDOW

Natural light and a view to the outside are important in the bathroom. Our first understanding of the weather and the general look of the day comes through the window.

Ideally, windows are on at least two sides of the room to provide even daylighting. If privacy is an issue, make multiple windows face a courtyard garden, perhaps with an outdoor shower. If you have room for only one window, place it where it illuminates the portion of the room that you see when you enter.

## 4. FROM THE LEAST INTIMATE PLACES TO THE MOST INTIMATE PLACES

Another principle that applies to residential design in general and to the bathroom in miniature is "the intimacy gradient." Just as you locate the bedrooms the farthest from the front door, you should locate the most private part of the bathroom the greatest distance from the entry to the room. The most private part varies from family to family, with the toilet being the most private for some and the bath for others.

## The Intimacy Gradient Applied to the Bathroom

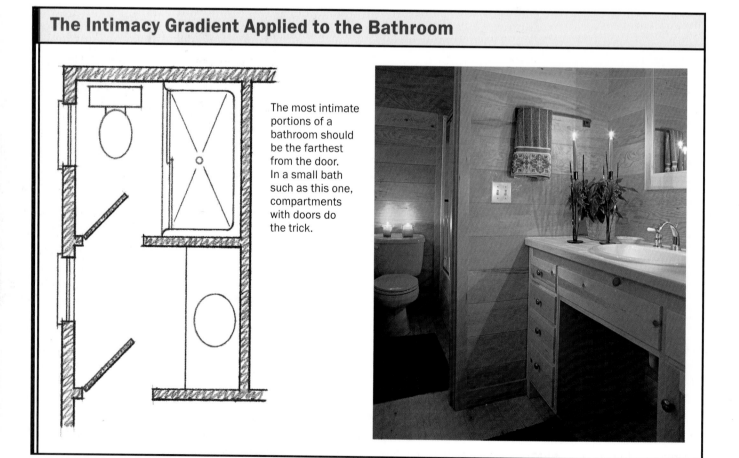

The most intimate portions of a bathroom should be the farthest from the door. In a small bath such as this one, compartments with doors do the trick.

**Diagonal sight lines enlarge a bathroom.** As seen from the shower, views across the tub and into the lavatory portion of this bathroom foster a sense of spaciousness.

For ventilation and a glimpse of the world at first light, a good window is a must in a bathroom.
Try to place it in a position that you walk toward in the room.

## 5. BORROWED VIEWS

In a small space such as a bathroom, it is difficult to get a direct view to the outside from each area. But it is possible to borrow the view across another space or another fixture. A shower is a good example. It needs to be enclosed with water-resistant materials. So a window in a shower with an exterior wall, particularly a beautiful wood window, is not an ideal candidate for part of a shower enclosure. There are a number of positions the shower can take in the bathroom that will allow for a good view through a clear-glass shower door.

## 6. PAY ATTENTION TO VERTICAL AND HORIZONTAL DIMENSIONS

Certain minimum clearances around bathroom fixtures are required by every building code. My own experience is that you need about 36 in. of elbow room at the lavatory to use it comfortably. Its counter is typically between 31 in. and 34 in. high. The rule: You want the water to run off your wrists, not your elbows. A double-lavatory arrangement is mostly ornamental unless it has 6 ft. of counter space.

A toilet compartment is tight at the code minimum of 30 in., about right at 36 in., and a waste of space after that. In fact, after 40 in., you lose touch with the walls on each side and the sense of enclosure they provide. Although the minimum dimension for a shower stall is 30 in., it must also have no less than 1,024 sq. in. of finished interior area. This amount is really minimal, and I wouldn't recommend less than 36 in. square, or a 30-in. by 48-in. rectangular shower if you can find the room.

The standard length for a tub is 60 in., and many are 66 in. or 72 in. long. If you get a deep, rounded-back claw-foot type, you can easily be comfortable with a 54-in.-long tub unless you're taller than 6 ft. I recommend, however, that you make an honest evaluation of whether you really ever use a tub and consider instead putting money into a nice shower.

| COMMON HEIGHTS OF BATHROOM FIXTURES ABOVE THE FLOOR | |
|---|---|
| Showerhead | 6 ft. 7 in. |
| Shower rod | 6 ft. 6 in. |
| Toilet-paper holder | 24 in. |
| Towel bars | 48 in. |
| Toothbrush holder | 48 in. |
| Soap holder | 48 in. |
| Tub-deck height | 18 in. |

Just as any good room benefits from a variety of ceiling heights, so does a good bathroom. Make the ceiling highest in the center, and lower it around tubs, showers, toilet alcoves, and window seats.

Any small room like a bathroom can benefit from the visually expansive effects of horizontal lines. This is often seen in traditional bathrooms as a strong cap on top of wainscoting. The lower part of the wall is done in a water-resistant finish such as tile or enamel paint and is capped by a strong horizontal band with plaster or wallpaper above. This horizontal band, combined with a baseboard and sometimes a crown molding at the ceiling, adds horizontal lines that visually enlarge the perimeter of the room.

Two vertical dimensions are often the subject of discussion and sometimes construction changes. The first is the height of sconces. I prefer a framed mirror above a lavatory with sconces on the sides because they give the best light to the sides of the face and fewer shadows in the facial recesses than does light from above the face. The height I use for sconces is the height of my client.

The last vertical dimension is one of those little details that gives me problems near the end of a project: the water supply to the toilet. Place it high enough, including the escutcheon, to be out of the baseboard. I've found that 10½ in. are enough to clear all but the tallest baseboards and still leave room for a flexible connection to the toilet tank.

*Nothing can replace cast iron for quietness in a drainpipe that comes down the wall of a first-floor living space.*

**To protect a wood floor from moisture damage,** the toilet sits on a marble slab.

### 7. WATER-RESISTANT FINISHES

There is probably nothing nicer than ceramic tile in a bathroom. Properly installed, it is a cleanable, water-resistant surface for floors, walls, and shower enclosures. If a whole wall need not be water resistant, ceramic tile can also make a beautiful wainscot. On floors, it can be colder on the feet than other materials, but a simple area rug or a more expensive heat pad under the tile can easily solve this objection. Too much tile can change the acoustics of a room, and you should keep to softer materials on the ceiling and a portion of the walls (or have lots of bars for big fluffy towels).

I have used wood floors in many bathrooms, and with today's tough floor varnishes, they can hold up well to a modest amount of water as long as it is not allowed to sit on the floor for a long period of time. It seems a little uncomfortable putting a toilet directly on a wood floor, so I use a transition pad made of a scrap of granite or marble for toilets on wood floor.

Another attractive, traditional bathroom-floor material is linoleum. It is nothing like today's vinyl plastics. Again, proper installation is important for resistance to water.

The only wall surfaces that truly need to be water resistant are the shower walls. There are a variety of useful materials ranging from one-piece molded enclosures to wall-size sheets of materials to individual pieces such as tile. In every instance, installation is critical, particularly at joints, to the ultimate success of the material.

It is helpful to have an easily cleanable surface around the lavatory on the countertop and on the walls immediately around the sink. Ceramic tile is a good choice. Natural stone, polished and sealed concrete, and other nonabsorbent materials work well on both surfaces. On walls, a good-quality enamel paint on smooth plaster makes a cleanable, water-resistant finish.

### 8. FIXTURES THAT REALLY WORK

To me, good-quality bathroom fixtures mean enameled cast iron for tubs and china for lavatories. I recently remodeled the two bathrooms in my 1929 cottage. After 70 years, it was finally time to replace the original enameled cast-iron tubs. Cast iron and china are still so commonly used that the price difference between these quality fixtures and bargain fixtures is modest.

Good fittings such as faucets and tub/shower valves, however, are noticeably more expensive than run-of-the-mill fittings, sometimes as much as triple the cost. I use them, however, whenever I can afford to because over their life they are still a bargain when compared with average fittings that last a far shorter period of time. I also have to admit that there is no other faucet that gives me the pleasure of use as a classic Chicago™ or Rudge faucet. For finishes, stay with tried-and-true nickel or chrome without the plastic coatings. Someone's going to

No-frills, high-quality plumbing fixtures such as this Chicago faucet will last for generations.

Simple chrome towel rings and stainless-steel cover plates offer durability and classic good looks.

have these faucets in 50 years if you make the correct choice.

One piece of equipment that has improved during the past few years is the exhaust fan. They are clearly quieter than five years ago. Companies such as Broan® and NuTone® have ceiling-mounted, barely audible exhaust fans. Speaking of noise reduction, the newer "coexcel" ABS plastic drainpipe seems to be quieter than the older ABS. But nothing can replace cast iron for quietness in a drainpipe that comes down the wall of a first-floor living space. The slight increase in material cost is more than offset in the long run of the life of the house.

## 9. IMPORTANT ACCESSORIES

Light fixtures, towel bars, medicine cabinets, furniture, switch-plate covers, shower doors—there are hundreds of opportunities to make decisions about these kinds of details in a bathroom. My advice: Keep them simple and straightforward. Buy good quality that will last a long time. Keep them related to each other in design and materials, except for the occasional humorous surprise. Look for timeless qualities. Choose things that you want to live with. There is no reason you can't enjoy even the most mundane item in your bathroom.

## 10. THE LOST ART OF BATHING

The previous suggestions will help you to make the ordinary bathroom that you use several times each day a pleasant, enjoyable place. Sometimes, though, you want to go beyond that and experience the real pleasure of bathing. The deep relaxation of hot water, the peaceful pleasure of bathing with family or friends, and the therapy of quiet immersion in water are all aspects of the art of bathing. The oversize master bathrooms in the pseudomansions of the late 20th century only hint at this fundamental human need. The essence has been lost in the cheap materials typically used to build them.

To re-create this experience requires a deep, profound examination of the history and tradition of bathing and the environment needed to support it fully. My sense is that the quality of the room as a space—with places to sit around the perimeter, with good natural light and with good connections to a private outdoor space—are paramount to creating this experience.

*David Edrington* is an architect in Eugene, Oregon. Many of these principles are elaborations on guidelines published in A Pattern Language by Christopher Alexander.

## Sources

**Broan/Nutone Group**
926 W. State St.
Hartford, WI 53027
www.broan.com

**Chicago**
2100 S. Clearwater Dr.
Des Plaines, IL 60018
(847) 803-5000
www.chicago-faucet.com

**Waterworks™**
60 Backus Ave.
Danbury, CT 06811
(800) 927-2120
www.waterworks.com

# Accessible Bathrooms

■ BY MARGARET WYLDE, ADRIAN BARON-ROBBINS, AND SAM CLARK

**B**athrooms, despite the world of evidence to support the need for new products and plans, haven't changed. Tubs, toilets, vanities, and layouts continue to accommodate manufacturers, plumbing conventions, and "average" human beings rather than users of all sizes and abilities. While there are many new assistive bathing products on the market, they continue to be "special," which usually means they are more expensive. And they often still carry the label "handicapped."

Traditional designs and products say to the user, "Do it my way or go without." Go without a bath, go without the ability to use the toilet by yourself, go without your privacy. But there's no reason why all of us shouldn't have the safest, most accessible bathrooms we can build. For architects and builders, this means combining layouts and fixtures that people of differing abilities can use safely throughout their lives. In this article we'll discuss some ideas on achieving a higher degree of safety and accessibility in both bathroom design and bathroom fixtures.

## Designating a Bathroom's Role

There should be one full bathroom on each accessible floor of the house. In larger houses, there should be a bathroom in each section of the house. A two-story house that has a half-bath on the first floor and a full bath on the second floor won't help a household member who cannot climb stairs.

Unless finances are so tight, or the house is going to be so small that two baths are out of the question, plan for a minimum of two. Having two bathrooms solves several problems. First, one may be public, and the other private. A public bath should be placed so that it can be reached by guests without their having to walk through bedrooms or other private spaces within the house. A private bath should be located in the bedroom area of the house, where family members can reach it from the bedrooms without exposure to guests. Bathrooms should be situated so that they can be reached quickly and easily from the bedrooms at night, via the shortest, most obstacle-free route possible.

## Provide Enough Space

Bathrooms need to be planned so that they have sufficient clear floor space (at least 30 in. by 48 in.) in front of and/or adjacent to each fixture and for moving about the room.

The bathtub or shower should provide clear space and good handholds at both ends so that someone may move into it from a position of strength. Each toilet should be neutrally handed—located so that an individual in a wheelchair could move onto it from the right or the left or approach it straight on. Toilets that are enclosed in small walled-in areas force users to approach and mount them without assistance because there's no room for a helper to stand.

People who use wheelchairs and other assistive products (walkers, canes, crutches) need more floor space at the points of inter-action with the bathroom fixtures than peo-ple who do not use these devices. The points of interaction include where you enter and exit and where you operate faucets, drains, and such. The smallest bathroom that can accommodate a wheelchair and provide access to a toilet, a traditional-size bathtub (30 in. by 60 in.), and a lavatory is 37½ sq. ft. (5 ft. by 7½ ft.). However, for a person to reach the toilet from either side, a larger bathroom is necessary.

## Choosing Doors

Doors are great for privacy and for control-ling drafts, but beyond that they just get in the way. When studying floor plans, people often visualize the door but overlook the door swing. All doorways and passageways in the house should be at least 32 in. wide. Pocket doors are desirable for bathrooms. They don't take up floor space in the bath-room or in the adjacent area. If hinged doors are used, they should swing out from the bathroom, not into it. When the door swings out, someone will always be able to get into the bathroom to assist a person if necessary.

Bathrooms with two doors offer some advantages. A bathroom between a bed-room (private space) and the living area (public space) could have doors opening into both areas, making it both a private and a public bathroom. Also, one door could swing into the bathroom, and the other out, eliminating the problem of having a door opening into and blocking a hallway.

## Use Lots of Handholds

All bathrooms should have a generous sup-ply of grab bars or handholds. They should be put anywhere the bather, dresser, or groomer is likely to make a change in body position. A handhold can be a bar, a rail, a shelf, an armrest, a countertop, or a ledge.

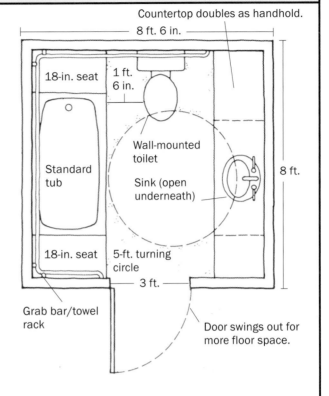

### A Small Wheelchair-Accessible Bathroom

Countertop doubles as handhold.

8 ft. 6 in.

18-in. seat

1 ft. 6 in.

Wall-mounted toilet

Standard tub

Sink (open underneath)

8 ft.

18-in. seat

5-ft. turning circle

3 ft.

Grab bar/towel rack

Door swings out for more floor space.

Although the spaces between these fixtures are fairly minimal, a wall-hung toilet and an open vanity enable a wheelchair user to approach the toilet from a side angle, and the bathtub offers seating at both ends.

*There's no reason why all of us shouldn't have the safest, most accessible bathrooms we can build.*

Handholds help support the weight of an individual while getting up or sitting down; they provide a steadying prop. Handholds should be capable of supporting up to 300 lb. They should not have any sharp edges, and they should not protrude into areas that are passages or that someone is likely to use for arm movement. Finally, they should be attractive. Handholds can double as towel bars, and some companies make entire lines of bathroom furnishings that add beauty and continuity to the bathroom decor.

## Toilets Are Too Low

The standard flush toilet isn't built to accommodate everyone, and using one requires strength and agility. Standard toilets provide no handholds to aid people in sitting down

or getting up. Yet many people don't have the strength to lower themselves to or raise themselves up from a seated position. The height of a standard chair is 17½ in. to 18½ in., but the seat height of a standard toilet is 15 in. to 15½ in. The lower height is almost impossible for some people to use. Some people need to approach the toilet from the side and will need a strong, sturdy handhold or surface on their preferred side to assist them in transferring or in lowering themselves to the toilet seat.

Many manufacturers offer "handicap" toilets with an 18-in. seat height. This is a good height for wheelchair users because most wheelchair seats are 18 in. to 19 in. high. A few entrepreneurs have developed toilets with seats that can lower and raise the user to and from a sitting position.

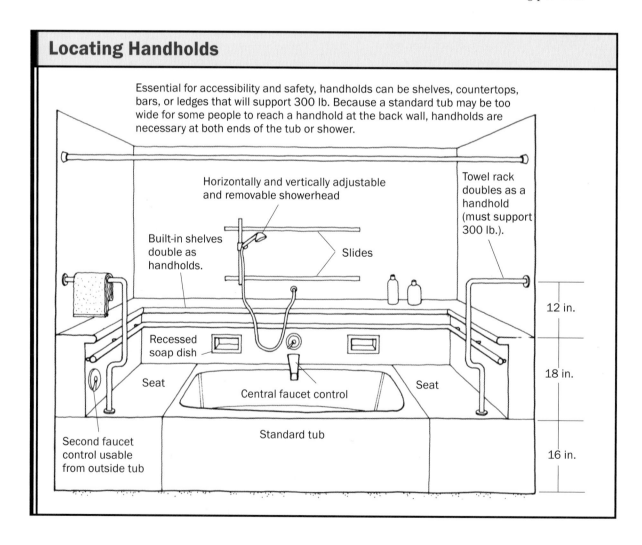

## Locating Handholds

Essential for accessibility and safety, handholds can be shelves, countertops, bars, or ledges that will support 300 lb. Because a standard tub may be too wide for some people to reach a handhold at the back wall, handholds are necessary at both ends of the tub or shower.

Horizontally and vertically adjustable and removable showerhead

Towel rack doubles as a handhold (must support 300 lb.).

Built-in shelves double as handholds.

Slides

Recessed soap dish

12 in.

18 in.

Seat

Central faucet control

Seat

Second faucet control usable from outside tub

Standard tub

16 in.

Finally, wall-mounted toilets are available that provide additional clear floor space and are easy to clean under. Many have flushing mechanisms that are easy to reach and to operate.

# Bathtubs and Showers

Bathing facilities need to be usable by people of all ages and abilities. They also need to be safe, fit extremes in body sizes from a small child to a very large adult, and be easy to clean.

Tubs with floors elevated to a height of 18 in. to 20 in. have several advantages. First, they make it much easier to bathe young children. You don't have to get down on your hands and knees; you can sit comfortably next to the tub in a chair. Raised tubs are much easier to clean. And there are some specialty tubs available that have doors or lifting devices, allowing for safer entry and exit.

The American National Standards Institute® (ANSI) has established standards that should be considered the bare minimum for safe, accessible bathtubs: a conventional tub equipped with handholds and an 18-in. seat at one end or an in-tub seat. The seat at one end must be at least 15 in. wide. There are no specifications for the in-tub seat except that it has to be able to bear bending stress, shear force, and tensile force of 250 lb. per sq. ft. on its seat and mountings.

All kinds of showers are available. A shower that offers good accessibility is a standard 3-ft. by 3-ft. shower unit with a 4-in. threshold, an 18-in.-high seat and abundant handholds (handholds all the way around the interior, handhold/towel bar on the outside and a sturdy seat). A shower seat should be at least 15 in. deep so that the user can sit on it without having to brace with the legs to keep from sliding out. The controls on a shower unit should be reached easily from outside of the shower enclosure.

## Bathtub Guidelines

The ideal bathtub may not yet exist, but here are some of the criteria that a good, accessible tub should meet:

- **Minimal risk of falling.** The tub should be designed so that the bather never has to stand in it.
- **Safe and easy entry and exit.** Handholds and support should be available at every turn.
- **Accessible plumbingware.** Faucet knobs and drain levers should be accessible from outside the bathtub or the shower. Everything should be easy to reach from whatever seated position a bather would take in the tub.
- **Recessed everything.** Faucets, faucet knobs, soap receptacles and shelving in and around the tub should not protrude into areas where elbows, heads, knees, or other parts of the body would come into contact with them.

# Sinks and Countertops

There are four basic types of bathroom sinks available: wall-hung, pedestal, legged, and drop-in. The wall-hung and pedestal sinks are usually freestanding. The wall-hung sink does not take up any floor space while the pedestal sink usually requires only a few square inches.

A lavish vanity and countertop can eat up valuable space that may be needed for maneuverability. A wheelchair-accessible lavatory needs to have about 29 in. of clearance from the floor to the bottom of the front of the sink. One compromise that allows for maneuverability, storage, and workspace is to build vanities that have an open space under the sink and drawer stor-

This shower unit is mounted flush with the floor, has a grab bar all around, and an 18-in.-high seat.

Accessible-bathroom gear doesn't have to look boring or sterile. This shower seat was designed to match the other components.

Wall-mounted toilets are easy to clean under and free up floor space. The grab bar is hinged to swing out of the way.

A power-elevating toilet seat lowers, raises, and tilts and it fits on a conventional toilet.

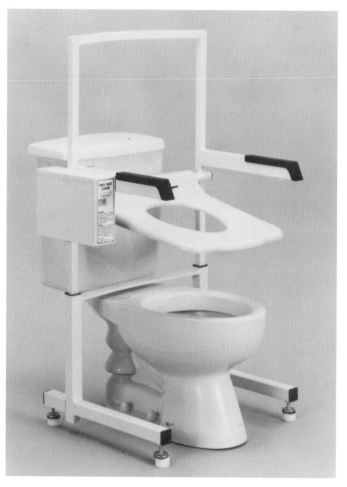

age on at least one side. If an open area under the sink is unappealing, removable vanity cabinets can be installed. On sinks that are open underneath, the drain and hot-water pipes should be covered or insulated to prevent a person from being burned.

Many ambulatory people do not wish to have the counter at the frequently used height of 30 in. because it requires them to bend over considerably to get their faces close to the water source. Individuals seated in a wheelchair, as well as people who would like to use the sink and grooming area while seated, are best served by 32-in.-high counters, with a sink-bowl depth that slopes from 3 in. at the front to about 5 in. to 7 in. to accommodate the user's legs. A height of 32 in. is a good compromise for tall, short, and seated persons.

# Plumbingware

Faucets and drain controls on bathtubs and showers should be located so that they can be reached easily from outside as well as from inside the tub. If, as in many homes, the bathtub is located right next to the sink or the toilet, the reach is greater because the user can't squeeze between the fixtures to reach the faucet or the drain. An ideal location for controls is on the wall near the outer edge of the tub.

Faucets should be easy to understand and to use. Some, unfortunately, have separate and confusing controls for the temperature and the water shutoff. Lever-handled faucets are much easier to use than round, cylindrical, or knurled knobs.

Handheld showerheads for the bathtub are delightful plumbing accessories, and they double as standard showerheads. Look for units that attach and detach easily, glide up and down the post, and offer a variable spray. Avoid systems with difficult-to-use knobs or small dials and controls.

Most sink faucets are outfitted with easy-to-use levers, but often the drain control is a

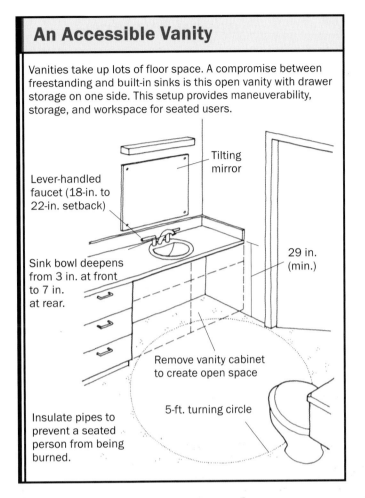

## An Accessible Vanity

Vanities take up lots of floor space. A compromise between freestanding and built-in sinks is this open vanity with drawer storage on one side. This setup provides maneuverability, storage, and workspace for seated users.

Tilting mirror

Lever-handled faucet (18-in. to 22-in. setback)

Sink bowl deepens from 3 in. at front to 7 in. at rear.

29 in. (min.)

Remove vanity cabinet to create open space

5-ft. turning circle

Insulate pipes to prevent a seated person from being burned.

tiny plunger located behind the spout. You need extremely nimble fingers to be able to reach and manipulate this control. An old-fashioned rubber drain plug on a chain would be easier to use. Sink-faucet sets should also be within reach. An easy, seated forward reach for women ranges 18 in. to 21 in. and for men 20 in. to 22 in. If the sink or the counter is particularly deep, the controls could be moved to one side of the sink to make them easier to reach. Another unconventional recommendation is to consider installing one of the new decorator kitchen faucets with a pull-out handheld spray in the bathroom sink. These are very handy for washing hair.

## TIP

*Bathtub and shower faucets and drains should be located near the outer edge of the tub where they can be easily reached from inside or outside the tub.*

## Sources

**Aqua Glass Corp**
320 Industrial Park Rd.
P.O. Box 412
Adamsville, TN 38310
(731) 632-0911
www.aquaglass.com

**HEWI**
2851 Old Tree Dr.
Lancaster, PA 17603
(717) 293-1313
www.hewi.com

# Nonslip Surfaces

Slippery flooring is a hazard in the bathroom and should be avoided. One important term for selecting suitable bathroom flooring, which is used by most flooring manufacturers, is the coefficient of friction (COF). Simply put, this is the amount of grip or resistance to slipping of a surface; the higher the number, the less slippery the surface. For instance, smooth concrete is very slippery when wetted with soapy water; its COF can be as low as 0.16. Ceramic tile, on the other hand, offers a pretty tenacious grip; when wetted with soap and water, its COF is as high as 0.59.

People vary in their demand for nonslip surfaces. People without mobility impairments can get by with coefficients of friction as low as 0.3, while people with mobility limitations, particularly those using assistive devices such as crutches, canes, walkers, and artificial limbs, need coefficients of friction ranging 0.7–1.0. Researchers at Penn State University estimated that 88 percent of the population would be "protected" by a coefficient of friction of 0.6 for flat surfaces and 0.8 for ramps (1:12 grade).

# Light, Mirrors, and Heating

A bathroom needs both natural and artificial light. Mold and mildew are less likely to grow in a sunny bathroom. Often bathroom windows are installed at a higher level than usual to ensure privacy. If this is the case, be sure that they can be operated from a height of 20 in. to 44 in. off the floor. Windows could be higher or lower, but make sure their handles are within this 20-in. to 44-in. "optimal-reach zone," or use electronic openers or install fixed windows.

Light is needed at the sink, the grooming mirror, and the bathing areas. At the sink, the light should be directed down toward the bowl. Be generous with light at the grooming mirror; light fixtures should be positioned on both sides and above the mirror. Incandescent or a warm fluorescent light is best at the mirror because it is closest to the spectrum of sunlight and will enhance the warm tones.

Bathrooms often have a single, fixed mirror over the sink. Consider installing a tilting mirror that pivots from the bottom and allows children and seated people the opportunity to adjust the mirror to their liking.

Scrutinize the built-in light in an enclosed shower. Will it provide adequate light for the aging eye when the shower is full of steam? Light over and around a bathtub should be equally distributed, nonglaring, and adequate so that the bather won't be confused by shadows or blinded by glare. Can the bather see to get into the tub?

Exhaust fans and in-room heaters are important accessories in bathrooms. An exhaust fan in climates prone to mold and mildew is an investment in the war against grime. Be sure to vent to the outside, not into the attic. An interior bathroom without a window or one located in cold climates should be equipped with a good exhaust system. Finally, in-room heating systems (infrared heat lamps or wall-mounted units) are important for people who have difficulty regulating their body temperature, particularly in cold climates. Keep towel bars away from coil wall-heater units, and locate these units where the bather is unlikely to fall or brush against them.

*Margaret Wylde, Adrian Baron-Robbins, and Sam Clark* are the authors of Building for a Lifetime, *a book about accessible home design, published by The Taunton Press. This article is adapted from that book.*

# A Gallery of Favorite Bath Details

■ BY CHARLES BICKFORD

**B**athrooms are busy little places. Unless you live on the space shuttle, you won't find a similar density of fixtures, wiring, and plumbing anywhere else in your house. Bathrooms must also reconcile contradictory design elements: They should be as waterproof as a locker room, yet be as comfortable as a living room. These basic requirements can make a tall order for any designer.

Fortunately, bathroom design can be exceptional. Bathrooms can cost a lot, but

with a bit of thought and less money, you still should be able to get a good bathroom. To find some ideas, I took an unscientific survey among architects, designers, and builders. The results are mixed regarding cost, but I hope all these projects give you food for thought for your next bathroom project.

*Charles Bickford* is a senior editor at Fine Homebuilding.

## SHOWERS WITHOUT BOUNDARIES

When clients requested a shower without a curb or door, Elliott & Elliott had to work out details that would confine water. A well-drained floor with a substantial pitch is the cornerstone of the design. A fixed 9-ft. by 4-ft. screen of acid-etched tempered glass blocks the spray. The shower's interior walls are covered with 1¼-in.-thick granite. Without a full enclosure, the shower throws small amounts of water on the floor, but usually no more than a normal shower.

*Bruce Norelius of Elliott & Elliott Architecture, Blue Hill, Maine*

### CUSTOM SINK

Powder rooms are often small because they need to contain only a toilet and a sink. The choice of toilets is fairly limited, so any leeway in design comes with the choice of sinks. If you can find someone to make the sink, you have even more choice. Paul MacNeely hired Boston metalsmith Henry Miller to design and create this small stainless-steel sink that saves space with an integral towel rack.

*Paul MacNeely, Jeremiah Eck Architects, Boston, Massachusetts*

## A VANITY THAT FITS THE SPACE

Because this powder room is narrow, Stephen Bobbitt originally chose a pedestal sink. But that meant less storage. Also, the clients were keen on using a custom-painted sink bowl. Instead, Bobbitt designed a cabinet with a shallow 18-in. depth and a curved front that takes up less room than a standard vanity. The pilaster motif and the slate-tile top are details drawn from cabinets in the nearby kitchen.

*Stephen Bobbitt, architect,*
*Seattle, Washington*

## CONTINUOUS BACKSPLASH

Without careful detailing, small bathrooms can feel cramped. One way to make a small room seem larger is to make the eye move around the room. To give a half-bath some visual interest, Sarah Susanka came up with an idea that extends the lines of the countertop backsplash around the room, much like a chair rail. Although made of tile in this example, the backsplash can be made of wood. This continuous line around the room is an effective means of breaking up a space; the room is divided visually into upper and lower halves, an arrangement that lends itself to contrasting paint or material schemes.

*Sarah Susanka, architect,*
*Raleigh, North Carolina*

## A SLATE TOWER OF SHOWER

When the great wide open calls, you have to go there. Or factor it into the design. The owners of this house spent a good deal of time in outdoor showers on Hawaiian vacations and liked that feeling of openness. When it came time to remodel their master bath, they asked Linder Jones to incorporate this feel.

The shower monolith is covered with 1½-in. thick slate over a plywood box bolted to the floor. Kneewalls of concrete and glass block on each side of the shower keep the splash factor to a minimum. Custom doors by BZ Design of Mountainview, California, open onto a private backyard.

*Linder Jones, Harrell Remodeling, Mountainview, California*

## CUSTOM MEDICINE CABINETS

Medicine cabinets that match the trim details of a bathroom are often overlooked in custom houses. David Edrington rights that wrong in a variety of ways. In this house, for example, he used the chair rail atop the wainscot as the bottom of the medicine cabinet, giving it sort of a window-stool-like appearance. The frame-and-panel door has a mirror for a panel, which is protected from behind by a piece of white plastic laminate. The doorknob matches those on the other bathroom cabinets, and the 1x4 trim around the cabinet is the same as that bordering the door to the room. Note the nickel-plated butterfly hinges. Small butt hinges would have worked just as well here, but European-style hinges would be out of place.

*David Edrington, architect, Eugene, Oregon*

## SHOWER-STALL WINDOW

Showers can be as dark and dismal as a cave. In-shower light fixtures are okay, but there's nothing like natural light, at least according to architect Keith Moskow. His solution to the problem: Install a window in the shower wall. Although he typically places the window in the exterior wall for the view, he used a small window in the interior wall of his own bathroom for the same effect.

But what about water damage to the window? Moskow's shower window is a fixed light that's reversed; the side meant to be exposed to the exterior is facing the inside of the shower. Moskow has also had good luck using casement windows with sills reconfigured to a 1-in-12 pitch. It's also advisable to use exterior-grade paint and/or clear varnish to protect the wood.

*Keith Moskow, architect,*
*Boston,Massachusetts*

## A TOWEL RACK AT THE EDGE OF A WINDOWSILL

In the midst of building a house, John Abrams and a business partner were designing fixtures and realized there wasn't much room for towel bars in the bathroom. One likely place was below the window, but the placement was too low. As they were looking into the room, job foreman Billy Dillon passed by and said, "We can just make the sill wider and cut a slot in it for the towels." As it turns out, the solution was nearly as easy as he made it sound. They widened the sill to extend 3½ in. beyond the casing and cut a 2-in.-wide slot in it. Screws concealed by plugs at each end of the sill keep the ends from cracking at the weak points.

*John Abrams, builder, Martha's Vineyard, Massachusetts*

## A HIDDEN SOURCE OF AMBIENT LIGHT

One of the hardest things to do is light a bathroom. Sometimes you need a lot of light, but sometimes you want only enough to navigate a path to the toilet. You certainly don't want to get into a staring contest with a light fixture at 3 a.m. While house-hunting, Nancy McCoy saw a detail that solved a handful of problems all at once.

In a small bathroom with a cathedral ceiling, partition walls separate the toilet, shower, and sink vanity. A 4-ft.-long fluorescent fixture mounted atop each wall is high enough to be hidden from view but bright enough to cast good ambient light over the room. Equipped with a daylight-balanced fluorescent lamp, the fixture is economical to operate and casts a warm-colored light.

*Nancy McCoy, lighting designer, San Francisco, California*

## WATER-SPACE FIREPLACE

During an extensive remodeling of a Minneapolis ranch house, the architects were transforming the study into a bathroom and the existing bath into a walk-in closet. The study's fireplace was in the middle of the wall and would be expensive to remove. A plan to cover the fireplace was discarded, so they decided to incorporate it into the new bath. In addition to a new tile border, the architects had Twin Cities artist Maureen Lyttle paint a design based on a local prairie-style landmark over the fireplace.

*Eric Oder and Ollie Foran, SALA Architects, Minneapolis, Minnesota*

SHOWERS ■ TOILETS ■ FAUCETS

**2**

# Choosing a Toilet

■ BY STEVE CULPEPPER

At first, the toilets in our house were merely sluggish. Then they got slower and slower until they didn't flush at all. But the toilets weren't clogged. Something was in the sewer line. So I rented a sewer snake, unscrewed the clean-out, and fed the hungry snake down the chute. In it went—10 ft., 25 ft., 40 ft. Still, the pipe didn't drain. As I pondered the problem, my young son stuck his head out the window, his little fists full of his favorite action figures, the Teenage Mutant Ninja Turtles®. "Turtles live in the sewer, Daddy," he said.

After the snake failed to hit paydirt, I retracted it and fed a garden hose down the sewer line. When the hose could go no farther, I turned up the pressure and just let the water eat. The hose had stewed in the sewer no more than five minutes when a dozen or so plastic Teenage Mutant Ninja Turtles, all horribly chewed by the sewer snake, burbled to the surface. I coiled up the hose and broke the news to my son.

## Gone Are the Days When We Could Flush Toys

After our sewer was deturtled and the attendant blockage removed, our toilets flushed magnificently. What was amazing was that all those Teenage Mutant Ninja Turtles could ever have been flushed down the toilet at all. But those were the days of the 5-gal. flush. With that much water chasing after them, an entire flotilla of Ninja Turtles could've been flushed home at once—and might have been.

Times have changed since that unclogging. Toilet-flushing capacity dropped from 5 gal. to 3.5 gal., down to the current nationally mandated standard of 1.6 gal.

Our old 5-gal. toilets could flush turtles, cigars, feminine-hygiene products, bullets, Popsicle sticks, and an occasional diaper with little effort. The new 1.6-gal. toilets sometimes struggle to flush our humble daily loads of human waste. However, the law's the law, as those who favor the law are fond of saying. And the law is the National Energy Policy Act of 1992, which requires that all toilets made or sold in this country

26

## What Makes a Gravity Toilet Flush?

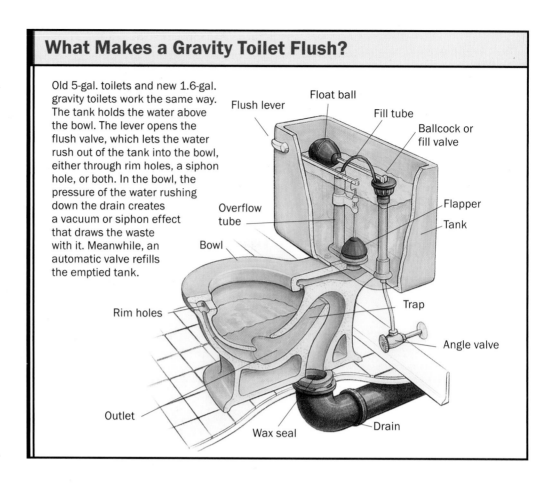

Old 5-gal. toilets and new 1.6-gal. gravity toilets work the same way. The tank holds the water above the bowl. The lever opens the flush valve, which lets the water rush out of the tank into the bowl, either through rim holes, a siphon hole, or both. In the bowl, the pressure of the water rushing down the drain creates a vacuum or siphon effect that draws the waste with it. Meanwhile, an automatic valve refills the emptied tank.

Flush lever
Float ball
Fill tube
Ballcock or fill valve
Overflow tube
Flapper
Tank
Bowl
Rim holes
Trap
Angle valve
Outlet
Wax seal
Drain

meet new federal water-efficiency standards. To conserve water, those standards set the upper limit of a single flush at 1.6 gal. The law took effect in 1994 for residential toilets and in 1997 for commercial toilets.

## How 1.6-gal. Gravity Toilets Work

Regardless of price or style, all gravity toilets depend on gravity to pull the water—and waste—through the system (drawing above). When the handle is pushed, a flush valve opens, and the water in the tank drains into the bowl, either through rim openings, through the large siphon-jet opening across from the drain at the bottom of the bowl, or through a combination of both. The gravity-fed speed of the water pushes the waste through the trap and into the drain.

But not all gravity toilets work the same way. For instance, there are different ways of ensuring that only 1.6 gal. of water are used

in a single flush. A few toilets use tank dams that fit around the flapper and allow only 1.6 gal. of water to flow into the bowl. Some toilets rely on an adjustable ballcock to cut off the flow of water after 1.6 gal. have flowed. On others, the flapper valve closes early. And still others include a plastic bucket-type device inside the tank that lets only the top 50 percent to 75 percent of water in the tank pass through during a flush. That height increases the head pressure of the water going into the bowl and results in a brisker flush.

However, most of these tanks hold more than 1.6 gal. of water, and most of the ways manufacturers control the flow of water from tank to bowl are open to adjustment. James Sargeant is a registered plumbing designer, master plumber, and director of the Wisconsin Plumbing Bureau. He's a member of the American National Standards Institute (ANSI) Toilet Adjustability Committee and is also in charge of codes and standards for the Kohler® Company. "Some plumbers have the notion that when they get the toilet from the factory, they have to adjust something, which wreaks havoc," according to Sargeant. "What they're adjusting is the water action. On a 1.6-gal. water closet, the bowl and trap way are a finely tuned design system to go with a specific amount of water. That's not just Kohler, that's all toilets. They're well-engineered bowls."

Despite the best efforts of engineers, designers, and manufacturers, plumbers and the general public still haven't gotten used to 1.6-gal. toilets and aren't happy with the way they flush.

## What This Country Needs Is Plunger Lessons

Complaints against the 1.6-gal. toilet include sluggish or incomplete flushing; a small "water spot," as the area of the toilet-bowl water surface is called; staining; and the need to double-flush or triple-flush. Critics say that if a 1.6-gal. toilet is flushed more than twice, it uses more water than the now-illegal 3.5-gal. toilets.

"In my opinion, it wouldn't be using more water if we went back to the 3.5-gal. flush because my customers are flushing more than two or three times anyway," according to Seattle plumber Hill Daugherty. "Everybody with a low-flush toilet has a plunger. The high-end houses have a decorative one, and the low-end houses have a regular plunger."

Terry Love of Love Plumbing & Remodel in Redmond, Washington, says, "Most customers who get 1.6-gal. toilets for the first time have to learn to use a plunger, and believe it or not, a lot of people don't know how to use a plunger."

According to Love, there's a right way to plunge a toilet. "Put the plunger in with water in bowl, and after a series of short, quick strokes, pull up until everything sucks down. Usually people do big strokes up and

down. Using that method, some blockages won't move."

If you don't like the way 1.6-gal. gravity toilets flush, you can't necessarily buy your way out of the problem. From plumbers around the country, I'm told that high cost isn't a guarantee that a 1.6-gal. gravity toilet will work well. Often, higher cost is really associated with fancy design, casting, or color more than with the quality of function. According to Rex Cauldwell, a plumber in Copper Hill, Virginia, "The brands that work well have nothing to do with the price of the commode. We're talking about some $75 toilets that flush better than $250 toilets."

Daugherty agrees, sort of. "With a lot of high-end toilets, you're paying for design. You can spend $1,400 or buy a lower-end toilet that will do the same thing."

Although plumbers and the public complain about the way new toilets flush, plumbing regulators say that the latest generation of 1.6-gal. toilets works just fine. What the public needs isn't more water but more education, they say. We have to learn that toilets are only for No. 1, liquid waste, and No. 2, fecal waste.

## These Toilets Are Here to Stay, So We'd Better Get Used to Them

Patrick Higgins is a licensed plumber and chairman of the ASME/ANSI Plumbing Fixture Committee. Higgins has a great deal of personal and professional experience with 1.6-gal. toilets.

"I've lived with 1.6-gal. flushes for about eight years," according to Higgins. "Every six months, I retrofit a different-style toilet off the shelf into my office bathroom, and I've yet to run into one I don't like. Kohler, Briggs®, American Standard®, Mansfield®, Gerber®. Someone's bringing a Toto® by next week. In my office bath now, I've got a combination water closet and bidet—that's a Geberit and it works like a gem. I've looked at all of them. It's a matter of getting used to

*Complaints against the 1.6-gal. toilet include sluggish or incomplete flushing; a small water spot; staining; and the need to double-flush or triple-flush.*

## What Else Goes into Toilets?

To see what goes into toilets (before what normally goes into toilets goes into them), I visited several toilet plants. I saw a wide range of manufacturing styles, from toilets made by hand in Wisconsin to an assembly-line plant in Ohio to an automated toilet plant in Georgia.

Believe it or not, toilet making contains some highly guarded proprietary secrets. Although I could observe any part of the process, I could photograph only certain production areas. Secrets range from the brand of robot used to spray glazing on the unfired toilet to the way the rim holes are punched or drilled in the green-clay toilet bowl.

Each toilet starts with several molds, depending on the model. Each mold is filled with slip, or liquid clay, and run through a dryer before being glazed and kiln fired. Afterward, the tank components are installed.

As important as the manufacturing process is, however, it's the research and engineering that go into the toilet and the final testing and quality control after manufacturing that make a truly good toilet.

Residential toilets must pass a series of ASME/ANSI tests, including a test in which 100 ¾-in.-dia. plastic balls are flushed; a granule test in which 2,500 tiny plastic granules are flushed; a test in which ink lines are drawn inside the upper rim and flushed away; a dye test; and a drain-line transport test.

Every manufacturer tests toilets coming off the line. However, many manufacturers have created their own tests in addition to the ASME/ANSI requirements. One company that has its own set of standards is Toto, the world's largest plumbing-products manufacturer. At the Toto toilet factory in Morrow, Georgia, an engineer tests toilets in a remarkably real way. He doesn't actually defecate in them, but it's close. Using a proprietary ingredient that closely resembles human feces, the engineer measures out up to 400g of this faux waste and then molds it into its familiar tubular shape.

After plopping the artificial waste into the toilet, the engineer wads up toilet-paper balls and drops them in on top of the bogus poop. The purpose of this realism is to ensure that the toilets meet or exceed ASME flush standards.

the product and not using the toilet as a wastebasket."

One reason that people still harbor ill feelings against 1.6-gal. toilets is that the early models were not up to the duty. Although manufacturers saw the new ultra-low-flush regulations coming, they were caught with their pants down when the government finally acted. Some early 1.6-gal. efforts were lamentably short of the mark. Cauldwell said he once got a letter from a major toilet manufacturer "apologizing for the fact that their 1.6-gal. toilet didn't work well but that they were required to make it."

# Sometimes the Problem Is in the Pipes

A number of plumbers warned me that installing a 1.6-gal. gravity-flush toilet in an old house could lead to clogs and backups. Often, older waste pipe is 4-in. or greater diameter cast iron, which is a lot rougher on the inside than modern plastic pipe. When the cast-iron pipe was installed, toilets flushed anywhere from 5 gal. to more than 7 gal. of water. But now that they're down to 1.6 gal., that's often not enough water to power the waste through.

"Houses that have 4-in. to 6-in. cast-iron drains are a problem," said Daugherty. "When you put a 1.6-gal. toilet in with that diameter pipe, it just barely makes the bottom of the pipe wet. As a retrofit in a house with old plumbing, it's lousy. Now I run high-use fixtures, like the washing machine, just after the toilet. The washing machine will help move that waste down the line."

Washington, D.C., plumber Ken Goldman believes that retrofitting 1.6-gal. toilets is the biggest source of problems plumbers have with the new fixtures. "We're using plumbing fixtures that were designed for the 1990s and putting them in plumbing systems that were designed for the 1920s," Goldman said.

# Power-Assist Toilets Blast the Waste Away

If old pipes are your problem, you may be interested in the power-assist toilets that many toilet makers now offer. These are toilets that use compressed air to force the waste down the trap.

Although a few power-assist toilets require compressors, most use the pressure of the home's water supply to get the job done—with the help of a pressure tank. The Sloan Valve Company's Flushmate® Flushometer is the industry leader in toilet pressure tanks. New on the market is the PF/2 Energizer® System from W/C Technology Corp.

Both work similarly: Water from the supply line is forced into the air-filled pressure tank at the house pressure of 60 psi or so, which compresses the air and exerts force on the water in the tank. When the flush button is pushed, the water jets into the bowl.

One benefit of a power-assist flush is that the water is contained inside the pressure tank, which is inside the china toilet tank. That insulation results in little or no tank sweating. Drawbacks include noise and price: Power assist generally adds $100 or so to the cost of a toilet.

Water rushing from the pressurized tank can be quite loud and startling. However, Bruce Martin, the engineer who developed both pressure-assist systems (he sold the Flushmate technology to Sloan), said his new PF/2 Energizer is much quieter than the Flushmate. "It's as quiet as a gravity toilet," he said.

Currently, only about 5 percent of toilets sold contain any type of pressure tank. Martin said the price of power-assist toilets will decrease, thanks in part to competition and volume sales. For now, only specially designed toilets can accept pressure-assist units. Martin is working on an adapter unit to convert ordinary gravity toilets to pressure assist.

# A Breakthrough in the Engineering of Gravity Toilets

One of the more promising developments in gravity-flush toilet design is the new vacuum-assist technology, which was developed by Fluidmaster® and is currently featured in the Vacuity® toilet manufactured by Briggs Industries.

Although on the outside the Vacuity looks like any other toilet, it solves several different problems that are common to many of the 1.6-gal. toilets. First, it contains two plastic tanks within the toilet tank that hold only 1.6 gal. of water between them. If it's modified to flush more, it won't flush, according to Oscar Dufau, Fluidmaster's product manager. The tanks also prevent the exterior china tank from sweating in hot, humid weather.

More important, the system allows the toilet to give a complete, clean flush using only the rim holes inside the upper toilet bowl. There is no siphon-jet hole in this toilet. With all the water that is coming out of the rim holes, the bowl stays cleaner.

The Vacuity is different from other gravity-flush toilets in another significant way. The Vacuity has two internal tanks and is configured in such a way that when you flush, a vacuum is created that powers the water into the bowl.

Although Briggs is the only U.S. toilet maker now using the Fluidmaster vacuum-assist technology, other U.S. companies are developing toilet prototypes that also use the technology. To keep the price of the unit at profitable levels, however, Fluidmaster has agreed to allow only four U.S. makers to license the technology.

Briggs lists its two-piece Vacuity toilet at near $300. However, I called around southern Connecticut and found a supply house that could order one for $217, plus $12 for the seat.

*It's the research and engineering that go into the toilet and the final testing and quality control after manufacturing that make a truly good toilet.*

The Toto Prominence toilet with the Zoë Washlet seat offers a warm-water spray, a prewarmed seat, and a fan with a filter to help clear the air.

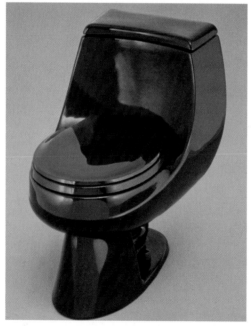

Kohler offers the Peacekeeper accessory on its toilets. There is no flush valve with the Peacekeeper; the only way to flush the toilet is to lower the seat.

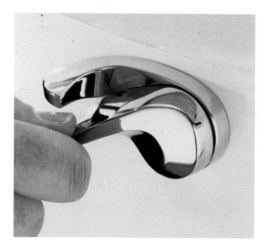

The Kohler Eco Lite offers two different flushes. Depending on the type and size of the load to be flushed, one handle flushes 1.1 gal. of water, and the other flushes 1.6 gal. of water.

# Special Toilets for Specific Needs

Within the wide range of 1.6-gal. toilets on the market are some fairly specific toilets and toilet accessories. These perform certain functions that you won't find on a run-of-the-mill fixture.

For instance, there is the ShowerToilet® by Geberit, a wall-hung fixture that contains a wand to give you a warm-water nether shower. The Geberit follows the shower with a flow of warm air. The Zoë Washlet® by Toto is a high-tech toilet seat that contains a heating unit, a fan, an air purifier, and a wand that sprays warmed water on your undercarriage (photo top left). The Washlet also offers a prewarmed seat. And both the Geberit and the Toto offer fans that extract toilet air and pass it through a filter.

But that kind of luxury comes at a price. The Geberit ShowerToilet, which has the tank and flushing mechanism inside the wall, sells for $4,200 in white. Color models cost much more. And the one-piece Prominence toilet by Toto, including the Zoë Washlet with heated seat and a remote-control device for controlling the spray, sells for about $1,200. Newer Toto toilets will come with an antibacterial glazing, which the company says inhibits the growth of germs and kills common types of bacteria.

Another specialized-toilet option is the Peacekeeper by Kohler. There is no flush lever or button on toilets equipped with Kohler's Peacekeeper technology (photo center left). Instead, it automatically flushes when the seat is closed, which makes it clear how it got its name. Here in Connecticut, Kohler's Wellworth toilet with the Peacekeeper installed retails for about $273 in white.

Kohler also makes the Eco Lite (photo bottom left), which replaces the standard single-flush lever with two levers. Depressing the smaller one gives a 1.1-gal. flush. Depressing the larger one gives a 1.6-gal. flush. The Eco Lite sells for about $186.

# Toilets That Don't Require Sewers or Septic Tanks

Say you want to build a house on a big rock. You'll rely on solar collectors for electricity. Rain will supply your water. But you can't build a septic system. So your choices are either to buy a composting toilet or an incinerating toilet, to store waste in a tank, or to hold it until you get off the rock.

If your concerns include the price of a septic tank and leaching field, the fate of the planet, or a tight water supply, your best bet is probably a composting toilet, of which there are a variety on the market. These include BioLet®, Sun-Mar®, Phoenix, and Clivus Multrum®.

A composting toilet works like the compost pile in your backyard. A carbon-rich material such as rice hulls or sawdust is added to the human waste. The materials then are mixed together in the composting unit, where they decompose together.

As to getting your composting toilet approved, the local health department usually has jurisdiction. Some jurisdictions recognize and approve composting toilets; others take them on a case-by-case basis.

## Composting doesn't come cheap

Prices for composting-toilet systems are generally pretty steep. A midsize Phoenix system, which includes two toilets and a basement-style composting unit, begins at about $4,600 installed, with vents and chutes, according to Glenn Nelson, who designs composting systems.

Small, self-contained composting toilets, such as the BioLet XL, sell for about $1,600. This toilet uses a 110v household current to power a heater (the rate of composting doubles for every 18°F increase in temperature), has a mixer motor and fan, and has a use capacity of four people. It needs venting just like the big composting units.

The Incinolet is a self-contained unit that burns waste. For four-person use, a 120v, 1,800w Incinolet® CF costs about $1,500.

An Incinolet uses electricity to incinerate human waste rapidly, leaving an odor-free ash that can be dumped with the trash.

In the Phoenix® system, a conventional composting toilet must be installed directly above the basement composting unit. Another type of toilet, the foam flush, can be installed at an angle away from the basement unit.

This self-contained BioLet composting toilet contains an automatic mixer, a heating element to accelerate composting, and a fan to draw odors up the vent.

Eljer's Triangle Ultra 1.5-gal. toilet is built for corner installation. With its triangular tank at a 90-degree angle, the Triangle Ultra fits neatly in a corner.

This wall-mounted toilet, the Kimera by American Standard, discharges to the rear so that no floor drain is needed. The rear-discharge feature is useful for remodels, where installing a floor drain would be impracticable.

The Nautilus II Water Closet is made in England, and it is sold in the United States by Burgess International for about $3,000 in white.

The Triangle Ultra by Eljer® is a 1.5-gal. toilet with a specially designed triangular tank that can help to solve your bathroom-space problems. With its 90-degree angled tank, the Triangle Ultra can fit into an odd corner of your bathroom. The Triangle lists for about $339 in blue (photo top left). In white the price for the Triangle falls to $269.

A few companies make wall-mounted, rear-discharge toilets (photo center left). These toilets are especially handy during a renovation when there's no practical way of installing a standard floor drain. The tank and flushing mechanism for these toilets are concealed inside the wall. However, because they are wall mounted, they require extra-beefy support inside the wall.

In our grandfathers' day, many toilet tanks were mounted high on the wall above the bowl. Because of that height, the water came rushing down into the bowl with enough pressure to force nearly anything down the drain. These old-fashioned toilets now use 1.6 gal. of water and are still available. Barclay® makes one in white that retails for about $850.

For those who feel at home on a throne, there's the English-made Nautilus II (photo bottom left), which is sold in this country by Burgess International. This is a real royal flush. A white Nautilus II sells for $3,000; in black, the price increases to $4,500. The mold for this lion-shaped commode is so complex that only 16 out of every 100 toilets survive the casting process.

For extremely specific toilet requirements, Toto makes a toilet that analyzes your urine, takes your blood pressure, and then sends that information to your doctor via a built-in modem. Unfortunately, you have to go to Japan to buy one.

# Which Toilet Should You Buy?

According to Patrick Higgins, all toilets that pass the ASME standards tests should work the same. In theory, I guess that's true. But we all know that standards are only part of the story. The true test of whether a toilet—or anything—works as it should occurs in the real world.

I can't definitively tell you which toilets work and which don't. All the plumbers I talked to had wildly differing opinions about which is the best gravity-flush toilet. There are a few other things to consider before spending money on a new commode.

Thomas Pape, chairman of the Indoor Plumbing Committee for the American Waterworks Association Conservation Committee, suggests that homeowners buy rounded-bowl toilets instead of the elongated variety. "These just seem to work better than the elongated bowl," according to Pape. "That's especially true in a setting that might be abusive. You get a better vortex action out of a round bowl."

A new feature of modern toilets is the advent of one-piece toilets, which cost more than two-piece toilets because they're harder to make. Otherwise, there is no significant difference between one-piece and two-piece toilets. They all flush the same way. In fact, some plumbers argue that the higher-tank two-piece toilets actually flush better than the more expensive one-piece models because the water in the tank flows into the bowl from a greater height and therefore has greater head pressure to accomplish a thorough flush.

Another thing that separates cheaper gravity-flush toilets from the more expensive ones is color. Color adds a lot to the price of a toilet. For instance, if I'm willing to make do with a plain white Kohler Rosario one-piece toilet, I can buy it at my local home-supply store for $296, plus the cost of a seat. If I want it in gray, that price increases to $455. American Standard's one-piece Ellise toilet in white costs $720. Make it black, and it increases to $1,005.

*Price estimates noted are from 1997.

*Steve Culpepper is a former* Fine Homebuilding *magazine and book editor. He is currently editorial director for the shelter subsidiary of Sabot Publishing.*

## Sources

**Advanced Composting Systems®**
195 Meadows Rd.
Whitefish, MT 59937
(406) 862-3854
www.composting-toilet.com
*The Phoenix*

**BioLet USA, Inc.**
150 East State St.
P. O. Box 548
Newcomerstown, OH 43832
(800) 5BIOLET
www.biolet.com

**Briggs Industries**
300 Eagle Rd.
Goose Creek, SC 29445
(800) 888-4458
www.briggsplumbing.com

**Burgess International**
647 Manufacturers Dr.
Westland, MI 48186
(734) 729-9306
www.burgesscabinetry.com

**Clivus Multrum**
15 Union St.
(800) 4-CLIVUS
www.clivus.com

**Eljer Plumbware Inc.**
14801 Quorum Dr.
Dallas, TX 75254
(972) 560-2000
(800) 423-5537
www.eljer.com

**Geberit**
1100 Boone Dr.
Michigan City, IN 46360
(219) 879-4466
www.us.geberit.com

**Incinolet**
2639 Andjon
Dallas, TX 75220
(800) 527-5551
www.incinolet.com

**Kohler**
444 Highland Dr.
Kohler, WI 53044
(800) 456-4537
www.kohler.com

**Sloane Flushmate**
30075 Research Dr.
New Hudson, MI 48165
(800) 533-3450
www.flushmate.com

**Sun-Mar Corporation**
600 Main St.
Tonawanda, NY 14150
Or
5035 N. Service Rd., Unit C9
Burlington, Ontario
L7L 5V2
Canada
(800) 461-2461
www.sun-mar.com

**Toto**
1155 Southern Rd.
Morrow, GA 30260
(800) 938-1541
www.totousa.com

**W/C Technology Corp.**
37685 Interchange Dr.
Farmington Hills, MI 48335
(888) 732-9282
www.wctc.com

# How to Install a Toilet

■ BY PETER HEMP

**WARNING!**
Following the installation instructions and using the hardware that accompany this toilet can lead to premature failure of the toilet, and structural damage to the subfloor and framing members within close proximity of the toilet.

**D**o the cautionary words to the left sound a little harsh? I haven't actually seen that warning included in the directions that accompany new toilets, but it wouldn't be out of place. The blister packs and directions tucked away in the box routinely include details and components that will work for a while but won't stand the test of time. I guess the manufacturers haven't had to pull up a toilet that began to seep after a few years. I have—lots of them.

A toilet failure is really a shame because with just a little bit of additional work, you can add years of service to the toilet and protect the structure that supports it. After going through the process many times, I've worked out a good method for installing a close-coupled toilet in new wood-frame construction. This is the garden-variety two-piece toilet that's in almost every residential bathroom in the country. Close-coupled toilets are easier to install than one-piece toilets simply because they are easier to handle. You install the bowl first, then attach the tank. But you can also use the advice presented here to install any kind of toilet, be it a one-piece Kohler or a temperature-controlled Toto.

## Good Installation Begins with the Floor Framing

The first commandment of toilet installation: **The toilet shall not move.** By this, I mean it has to be connected to the floor as firmly as possible, and the floor has to be sturdy enough not to deflect when someone is sitting on the throne. This means that the ideal floor framing takes into consideration the placement of the toilet. If I get my way, the toilet's drain is centered between floor joists that are 12 in. o.c. with a pair of blocks flanking the drain line.

Framing doesn't always turn out this way, of course. And I will admit to having remodeled more than a couple of bathroom floor joists with my chainsaw to make room for drain lines. But I head off any joists that have to be removed and put blocking on both sides of the toilet flange. This blocking helps to distribute the weight of the toilet.

## Trim the Pipe and Install the Flange

When I became a plumber, toilet drains were made almost exclusively of cast-iron pipe. But now, most new homes are plumbed with ABS or PVC plastic. I used 4-in. ABS pipe in the demonstration job shown in these photos. Where I live in the Bay Area, you can also use 3-in. pipe for replacing existing 3-in. drain lines. But inspectors require 4x3 closet bends for connecting the toilet to 3-in. lines.

During installation, the toilet's drain line extends above the floor, where it is capped with a plastic plug to make a watertight seal for the leak test. When it's time to install the toilet, I knock out the plug with a hammer and trim the pipe flush to the finished floor.

Next, I install the closet flange, a fitting that links the toilet to its drain line. There are three common types of closet flanges: solid plastic, steel rim with a plastic hub, and cast iron. The all-plastic flange and

**A sturdy base begins with the floor framing.** A pair of blocks nailed to joists on 12-in. centers create a chase for the toilet's drain line. The blocking and closely spaced joists will minimize deflection in the subfloor. For standard toilets, the center of the drain line should be 12 in. from the finished wall.

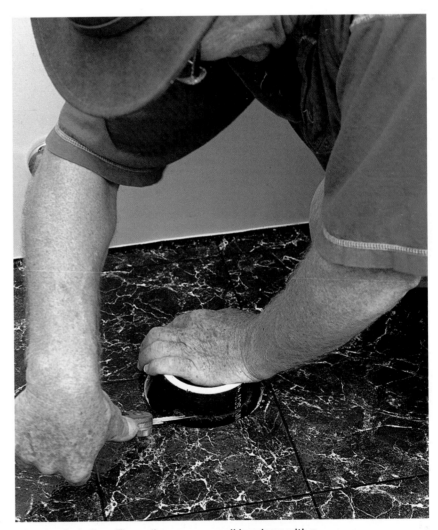

**Trim the drain line.** The author uses a small handsaw with a reciprocating-saw blade to cut the plastic drain pipe flush with the floor. The white ring atop the pipe is the remains of the test plug.

Affix the closet flange with noncorroding screws. Rotate the outer ring of the closet flange until the narrow portions of the slots on both sides of the ring are equidistant from the wall. Then attach the flange with brass or stainless-steel screws.

Secure the closet bolts to the flange. Slide the closet bolts into their slots, and orient the T-shaped head of the bolts so that they are perpendicular to the slots. Then tighten each bolt with corrosion-proof washers and nuts.

# Closet Bolts Anchor the Toilet

The second commandment of toilet installation: **Don't use hardware that can corrode in wet locations.** This hardware includes closet bolts, the long machine-thread bolts that fit into slots in the toilet flange and anchor the toilet to the floor. Chances are good that the bolts included with the toilet are brass-plated steel. Check them with a magnet. If they stick to it, don't use them. Same goes for the washers and nuts. Your local plumbing-supply store will have brass bolts and nuts, and stainless-steel washers. If you can find them, get the extra-long, 3-in. by ⅚-in.-dia. closet bolts.

Most instructions say to slide the bolts into the flange, put a wax ring on the toilet's outlet, and then lower the toilet onto the flange. There are better ways to do both. First, take the extra step of affixing the closet bolts to the flange (photo bottom left). This will ensure that the closet bolts won't spin when you bolt down the toilet.

# A Wax Doughnut Seals the Toilet to the Closet Flange

The bolts will keep the toilet firmly on the floor, but they won't keep sewer gases out of the room, or prevent seepage from the toilet from rotting the subfloor and the framing. That's what wax rings are for (top photo, p. 40).

Wax rings have been around for centuries. The English, who invented what has become the modern toilet, used beeswax to seal the connection between toilet and pipe. But as the newfangled toilets gained popularity, they outstripped bees' ability to make wax. Modern wax rings are made of vegetable and petroleum waxes, with polyurethane additives.

the combo plastic-hub/steel-rim flanges are cemented to the drain line and then screwed to the floor. This is a snap because there are plenty of countersunk holes for the screws and because the outer rings of these two types of flanges are large enough to achieve good bearing on the subfloor. Nevertheless, it's important that the drain-line hole in the subfloor be accurately cut and not too big. It's also best to have the finished floor in place before installing the closet flange. If the edge of the flooring abuts the toilet, it creates a crevice that is tough to clean. No matter what kind of flange you use, its lip should be securely fastened to the subfloor with stainless-steel or brass screws.

## Sunken Flanges, Broken Flanges

Remodeled bathrooms often get new floors, which means the flange is below its correct level for a standard wax seal.

The typical way to deal with this is to use a thick wax ring or a couple of standard wax rings, one without the plastic funnel, stacked atop one with the funnel. A better way to accomplish the same thing is with a closet-flange spacer. The best way is to use an Ultra Seal®, which can be adjusted up or down to deal with any floor thickness.

An Ultra Seal is a reusable fitting made of PVC plastic. Its bottom fits into the drain line, where it is sealed by an O-ring. At the top, a rubber boot fits around the horn of the toilet. Unlike bowl waxes, an Ultra Seal can't migrate horizontally or be ruptured by water or air pressure from a toilet plunger. Ultra Seals aren't just retrofit devices: You can use them on new construction, too. They cost about $10.

If you're faced with a broken cast-iron flange, consider using a repair flange, such as #1012 Spanner® flange from Donald O. Smith Co. This slice of galvanized steel can save you a lot of trouble in the right circumstances.

A spacer raises the flange height. If a new floor puts the closet flange below floor level, you can get back on top with a PVC closet-flange spacer.

A fix for broken cast-iron flanges. You can repair a broken flange with a Span-It repair flange. Use the existing bolt holes to affix the new flange.

A wax-free toilet seal. Ultra Seal connectors use O-rings and rubber gaskets to make a fool-proof hookup between a toilet and its drain line. The grooves allow the O-ring to be adjusted for different pipes.

Wax rings work fine if they're installed properly. If they aren't, the toilet will leak. And using a plunger on a toilet to clear a blockage in the drain pipe can rupture a wax seal. My guess is that future plumbers will use wax-free seals. For now, wax rings are the standard.

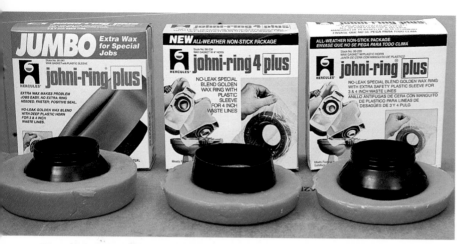

**Wax-ring choices.** Variables such as drain diameter and floor thickness influence your selection. The thick ring on the left accommodates the thickness of a new bathroom floor without resetting the closet flange. The other two rings are for 4-in. and 3-in. drain lines.

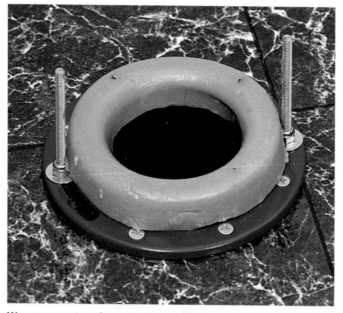

**Wax goes on top, funnel goes down.** Closet bolts secured and the wax in place, this closet flange is ready for its toilet bowl.

## Check the Toilet for Defects

If you didn't look over the bowl when and where you purchased it, it's now time to give it a good inspection before you install it. Keep the original cartons and paperwork in case you need to exchange a defective fixture. With toilet bowls, the main problems that you want to avoid are a deformed inlet, the opening between the bowl and the tank;

a crooked foot; or a deformed horn on the bottom of the bowl.

Contrary to what you might read on the box, the bowl wax should not be pressed onto the bottom of the toilet bowl. It should be installed on the closet flange (photo below). Often, the plastic funnels are not perfectly round and require some manipulation to get them to fit into the flange. You can't do this if the wax is stuck to the bowl. Waxes mounted to bowls can twist during installation, causing a partial blockage of the drain line.

## Set the Bowl

With the bolts and wax in place, the toilet bowl can be set. Here's where the extra-long closet bolts pay off. They are tall enough to act as locating pins for the bolt holes in the bowl without the projecting horn on the underside of the bowl nudging the wax out of position. Once both bolt holes have found their respective bolts, let the bowl settle onto the wax ring. The third commandment now comes into play: **Do not push on, sit on, or wiggle the bowl downward as it is set.** To do so will overcompress the wax, leading to a potential leak. Instead, use a wrench, alternating six or seven strokes from one nut to the other, until the bowl is snug to the finish floor.

If the closet bolts were installed in the proper plane, the bowl will be perpendicular to the plumbing wall. The holes in the bowl's foot are large enough to give you a little fine-tuning room if the bolts aren't perfectly positioned. Make this final adjustment just before the bowl is tight to the floor.

And just how tightly do you snug the nuts? If you overtighten them, you can crack the foot of the bowl. I suggest that you grasp the edges of the bowl and try to wiggle it. When the bowl remains motionless in spite of these efforts, call it done—for now. Usually the nuts will loosen a bit after the bowl has been in use for a while, and you might need to make a final tightening of the nuts.

For those installers who will be living with the newly installed toilet, this is no great inconvenience; you can check the nuts a few days after the installation. The professional installer has to take more risks and tighten the nuts to a greater degree on the first and—it is hoped—only visit. Either way, before you trim the closet bolts, you should install the tank. Many toilet bowls somehow pass the factory-testing procedure and leak soon after installation. If you need to lift the toilet and try again, you can reuse the same bolts.

# Installing the Tank

The typical two-piece toilet has two fittings on the bottom of the tank. The small one is the supply inlet, the fitting that connects to the angle-stop valve on the wall behind the toilet. The larger one is the flush-valve lock nut. I check them both to make sure they are tight before setting the tank on the bowl. A big, sponge-rubber gasket fits over the flush-valve lock nut (bottom

## Stainless-Steel Clips Instead of Plastic Washers

If your toilet includes plastic washers that act as retainers for the closet-nut caps, don't use them. These disks are time bombs. When someone sits on the bowl, their shifting weight compresses the soft plastic disks, which in turn causes the closet nuts to loosen. Then the bowl begins to move around, the wax seal fails, and seepage begins. Usually, the seepage goes on for a long time before it is detected and does a lot of damage. Just ask any termite contractor.

Instead of the plastic disks, I use stainless-steel clips. Ironically, the plastic disks were supposed to replace these clips. Most hardware stores still offer them, but make certain they are stainless steel.

**Stainless-steel clips retain the bolt caps.** Before drawing the bowl tight to the floor, the author slips a retainer clip and a stainless-steel washer over the closet bolt.

**Tank-bottom connections.** Using a portion of the shipping carton as a work surface, the author snugs tight the threaded connections. The wrench is on the flush-valve lock nut. The supply inlet is to its left.

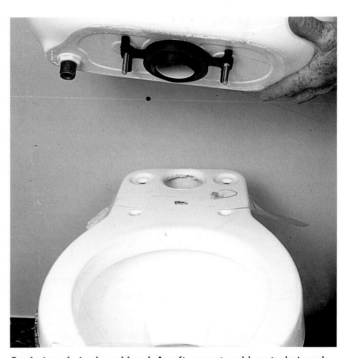

**Gasket weds tank and bowl.** A soft, sponge-rubber gasket seals the joint where a two-piece toilet comes together. The tank bolts project through the ends of the gasket.

**Putty blobs add insurance.**
Plumber's putty can help
to prevent leaks where the
tank bolts pass through
the bottom of the tank.
The washer is sandwiched
between the blobs.

**Prep the bowl's inlet.** A bead
of silicone grease around the
edge of the inlet can stop a
leak before it starts.

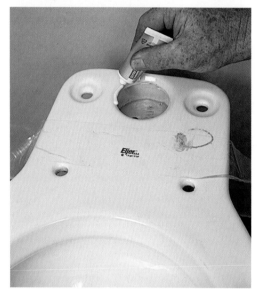

**Tighten down the tank.** Hold
the tank bolts steady with a
screwdriver and tighten the
nuts from below with a socket
wrench. Don't turn the screwdriver. Doing so can deform
the rubber washers.

right photo, p. 41). Some toilets come with
this gasket preinstalled. Others let you do
the honors. Slip the gasket over the nut, and
then insert the tank bolts and their washers.
If your toilet has a tank float, take it out for
this part of the job. You'll be able to reach
the bottom of the tank more easily with it
out of the way.

As before, make sure the bolts are solid
brass. I wrap small gobs of plumber's putty
around the bolts on both sides of the washers. Next I run a bead of silicone grease
around the bowl's inlet. Pipe-joint compound will also work for this task.

Lower the tank into place, making sure
the bolts drop through the holes in the
bowl. Next, slide a brass or stainless-steel
washer up each bolt, followed by the brass
nut. Then align the tank to the wall so that
it is as parallel as possible and snug up the
nuts with a socket wrench and a long screwdriver. Tighten the nuts slowly, using the
wrench to turn the nuts. Alternate five or six
revolutions per side, until the tank rests
firmly on the bowl.

# Time to Hook Up the Water Supply

There used to be a real art to hooking up the
water to a toilet. A plumber had to custom-
cut a supply tube from brass or copper tubing and then bend it carefully to avoid
kinks. Each supply tube was a little different,
depending on the location of the angle stop.

Not any more. Hooking up the water is the easy part now that manufacturers have figured out how to make flexible supply hoses that don't burst. Called overbraid hoses, these supply lines have woven brass or stainless-steel sleeves over flexible plastic cores. Install the angle-stop connection first because these threads are harder to start. Then hook up the ⅞-in. coupling to the tank. If the hose is longer than necessary, you can make a loop out of the excess and tuck it behind the toilet.

Before turning on the supply, look in the tank and make sure that any tubing between the fill valve and the overflow tube of the flush valve is secured. There should be a little clip for this. Even secured tubes may come loose with the first filling of the tank. So be prepared to turn the water off abruptly.

It is a good idea to open the angle stop just a little bit at a time and fill the tank slowly until the fill valve shuts off automatically for the first time. Depending on the type of fill valve you have, you might need to adjust the water level to match the mark provided on the back wall of the tank. This mark might be just a scratch and the letters

Flexible hoses make supply hookup a cinch. The angle stop (supply valve), which provides water for the toilet's tank, should be about 6 in. above the floor and 6 in. to the left of the drain's center line. Loop any excess supply line behind the toilet.

WL in the china. Or it may be a painted word: Water Level.

Now you should flush the bowl a half-dozen times, and check for leaks at all the connections. If you've got a leak at the tank connection or in the supply line, tighten the nuts. If water accumulates around the bowl's foot and nothing else is leaking, you've got a problem with the wax ring, and you'll have to pull out the toilet and start over again. Once you've got a leak-free toilet, use a small hacksaw to cut off the closet bolts and install the caps over them. A sealant may be applied around the base to finish the job.

*Peter Hemp is a plumber living in Junction City, California. He is the author of* Plumbing a House *and* Installing & Repairing Plumbing Fixtures, *both published by The Taunton Press, Inc.*

## Sources

**Donald O. Smith Co.**
6424 Bandini Blvd.
Los Angeles, CA
90040
(800) 262-5011
www.dosmith.com
*Spanner flange*

**Predco**
13260 18 Mile Rd.
Rodney, MI 49342
(800) 323-6188
www.plum-bob.com
*Ultra Seal*

## To Caulk or Not to Caulk?

Should you run a bead of sealant around the base of the toilet and the finish floor? Many inspectors will demand it before they sign off. If you've got a 100 percent watertight marriage of bowl wax and closet flange, a caulking bead does no damage. But adding one immediately can be an expensive maneuver. Seepage that would soon appear at the edge of the toilet and warn you of such circumstances will never appear. Instead, accumulating liquid finds its way into the layers of flooring and causes damage.

# Plastic Tub-Showers

■ BY SCOTT GIBSON

**A**ny plumber in America contemplating three flights of stairs and a 350-lb. cast-iron bathtub would be happy to give you at least one good reason why someone invented the plastic tub-shower. Until the 1960s, a knee-buckling delivery of a heavy tub to a second- or third-floor bathroom was routine. When the plumber had finished hooking up the tub and shower, a tile installer would complete the job. The result was certainly durable, but the process took time and specialized skills. Plus a strong back.

Then came a boom in plastics. Steadily improving polyester resins, and better equipment to combine the material with chopped fiberglass, allowed the mass production of all kinds of things—boats, car fenders and panels for truck trailers, and plumbing fixtures. One-piece plastic tub-showers were light and relatively inexpensive, and they could be installed quickly. Later, manufacturers began making combination tub-showers from molded acrylic plastic reinforced with fiberglass.

Combination tub-showers are now made by dozens of companies, large and small, and in a variety of price ranges. The most elaborate models include a half-dozen showerheads, CD players, television screens, steam generators, and whirlpool jets (gazing at one of these aquatic entertainment centers at a Chicago trade show earlier this year, a dumbfounded observer wondered aloud, "Why would anyone ever get out of the shower?"). Most tub-showers are more basic than that.

No matter what the brand name or its features, a plastic tub-shower will be either fiberglass-reinforced plastic, what the industry usually calls FRP or Gelcoat, or molded acrylic plastic. In addition to one-piece fixtures, limited by their size to new construction, you may also choose a remodeler's tub-shower that is assembled from three or four separate pieces small enough to be maneuvered through a finished house.

Plumbers may not buy as many Doan's Pills® as they used to, but they are not universal in their praise of either gelcoat or acrylic tub-showers. Although manufacturers disagree, many plumbers don't think plastic tub-showers will last as long as cast iron and tile. One-piece plastic fixtures come in a few standard sizes that are harder to adapt to odd-size bathrooms. Plastic can

**Gelcoat is the thrifty standard.** Although more lavish models are readily available, this Gelcoat tub-shower is typical of fiberglass-reinforced bathroom fixtures designed as economical alternatives to traditional bathtubs.

**Right this way.** A clean polyester-resin mold for a fiberglass-reinforced tub-shower is rolled toward the start of the production line at the Aqua Glass plant outside of Memphis, Tennessee.

**First stop on the production line** is a Gelcoat spray booth where the mold is sprayed with an initial coat of resin. In later steps, chopped fiberglass twine is mixed with polyester resin to build wall thickness.

**Bubbles or voids in the fiberglass layer** will weaken tub-shower walls, so fixtures are thoroughly rolled out by hand after they are sprayed.

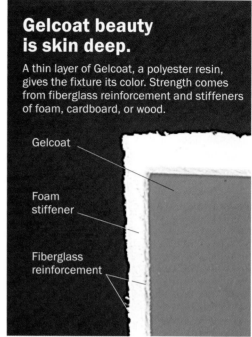

## Gelcoat beauty is skin deep.

A thin layer of Gelcoat, a polyester resin, gives the fixture its color. Strength comes from fiberglass reinforcement and stiffeners of foam, cardboard, or wood.

Gelcoat

Foam stiffener

Fiberglass reinforcement

be noisy, and it doesn't retain heat as well as cast iron. Even so, their seamless, no-leak design and advantages in weight and ease of installation have made plastic tub-showers as common as plastic-laminate countertops (for more on installation, see the sidebar on p. 48). And there's no getting around the lower cost. An acrylic tub-shower can cost about $1,000, rivaling the cost of a traditional installation. But no-frills Gelcoat models start at about $200 at big building-supply dealers.

## Gelcoat Is the Less Expensive, More Common Option

The plastic tub-shower owes its existence to a marriage of chemistry and assembly-line efficiency. A Gelcoat tub-shower is built from the inside out, beginning with a mold in the exact shape of the finished product (photo top left). The mold is a positive—the first layer of material applied to it becomes the finished side when the mold is removed. What goes on first is the Gelcoat layer, a special polyester resin that forms the smooth outer surface of the fixture (center photo, facing page). The Gelcoat layer determines the fixture's color. Manufacturers may apply Gelcoat a little differently (one coat or two, for instance), but this layer is essentially a paint film. When dry, it's 20 mils thick, more or less. Subsequent coats of chopped fiberglass and polyester resin are applied to what will be the back of the fixture, the part you never see. As soon as these laminating coats are applied, every inch of the fixture is rolled down by hand to squeeze out voids between the Gelcoat and the chopped fiberglass (bottom photo, facing page).

Between laminating coats, workers also apply wood blocks and other stiffeners to reinforce the tub floor and shower walls. Sheets of corrugated cardboard are a common choice for the stiffening material in tub walls, wood in the floors. I thought one manufacturer, Tennessee-based Aqua Glass, had a better idea—a layer of expanding polyurethane foam between coats of fiberglass chop instead of cardboard on shower walls. Foam reinforces the fiberglass, deadens sound and helps the tub to hold heat. No matter what material, it is covered by the next fiberglass layer.

After the last coat of fiberglass is applied, the tub-shower is popped off the mold and gets drain and overflow holes and a grab bar. Rough edges are ground down, and the fixture is inspected, packed, and then shipped. What the customer will get is a fiberglass-reinforced thermoset plastic shell somewhere between ¼ in. and ⅜ in. thick, weighing 125–145 lb. An economy-grade Gelcoat tub-shower is likely to be white or off-white with a simple grab bar and a molded ledge you can use as a soap dish. Spend more money, and you will get higher shower walls; a deeper, wider, and more comfortably molded tub; a greater choice of colors; and more elaborate contours and detailing in the shower walls. The basic fiberglass construction, however, probably will be the same. Standard tubs are either 45 in. or 60 in.

long, and from 30 in. to 42 in. wide. Heights typically range from 72 in. to 78 in. At the low end, a Gelcoat tub-shower is about $200. Although prices vary regionally, more elaborate models cost between $400 and $500.

## One Company Uses a Two-Part Mold to Make Fiberglass Fixtures

A variation on this theme is the Vikrell tub-shower made by Sterling®, a Kohler-owned company in Rolling Meadows, Illinois. These units are manufactured with the same ingredients as a standard Gelcoat tub-shower. But instead of laying up a fixture with several layers of chopped fiberglass and polyester resin, Sterling mixes resins, chopped fiberglass, coloring agents, and other ingredients and puts them in a big compression mold. Two halves of the mold are brought together, squeezing the material into its final shape. Sterling bought the patented process from Owens-Corning® in 1987.

Like Gelcoat, Vikrell is a thermoset plastic that will not change its shape with heat once it has cured. The company says that its tub-showers will not chip, crack, or peel because they are not laminated. Color is molded all the way through the unit. Structural ribs that are molded into the fixtures add rigidity and support, the company says. Vikrell fixtures are priced between Gelcoat and acrylic units. One key difference, however, is that the Sterling tub-showers are not available as one-piece units. They come only as four-piece units that include a tub and the three wall sections that snap together to form the wall surround.

*Their seamless, no-leak design and advantages in weight and ease of installation have made plastic tub-showers as common as plastic-laminate countertops.*

# When a One-Piece Fixture Is Just Plain Too Big

A fiberglass or acrylic tub-shower offers one hard-to-beat feature: Its seamless design eliminates potential leaks that cause havoc in the bathroom (and in ceilings below). The drawback is that a one-piece fixture must be moved into an unfinished bathroom during the early stages of construction. By the time walls are framed and doors are hung, it may be impossible to maneuver even a small one-piece fixture (72 in. high and 30 in. wide) through the house. So manufacturers also offer multi-piece, or sectional, tub-showers made specifically for remodels. These fixtures usually come in three or four pieces, all small enough to be maneuvered down hallways and through finished door openings. Once in the bathroom, the pieces are reassembled and installed.

Just like a shingled roof, a sectional tub-shower gets its watertightness from overlapping seams that channel water outward. When you're installing one of these fixtures, the tub goes in first, followed by panel sections making up the walls of the shower. Seams may be either horizontal or vertical. Nailing flanges on the top edge of the tub tuck behind wall layers so that water can't run behind the fixture.

Vikrell fixtures made by Sterling use a snap-together joint between wall sections that does not require any additional fasteners or caulk. More common are wall-seam joints that require at least some caulk plus screws or bolts to complete the seal. A top-quality silicone caulk is the sealant of choice.

If you want a new tub-shower, you could be excused for not wanting to tear out the tile walls and tub you already have. It's a dirty, time-consuming job complicated by the weight of a cast-iron tub and fairly

**An old tub gets a face-lift.** Chicago-based Luxury Bath Systems updates worn cast-iron bathtubs and aging tile walls with custom-molded acrylic replacements. No demolition is required.

elaborate plumbing. Luxury Bath Systems®, a Chicago-based company, pondered that dilemma and came up with an answer. For between $1,500 and $2,000, the company covers up the old tub and walls with a new acrylic shell. A local contractor measures your existing tub and orders a replacement.

**New tub in a day.** Foley installs a new tub in a day, a plus for clients unwilling to put up with construction delays.

**Acrylic is lightweight and easy to maneuver.** Connecticut contractor Paul Foley fits a new acrylic tub over a cast-iron fixture that will remain in place. The two are bonded with silicone caulk and butyl tape.

Back in Chicago, the company chooses one of the 400 vacuum molds it has on hand (they are made from old bathtubs) and produces a ¼-in.-thick acrylic shell. In about a day, the contractor fits this new skin over the existing tub, bedding it in butyl tape and silicone adhesive caulk, and installs acrylic-sheet shower walls. No tear-out is required.

If there's any question about water damage in existing walls, the contractor will tear out some of the existing tile walls and make sure the substrate is sound before the new surround goes in.

**An acrylic tub-shower has a roof.** Vacuum molding dictates the full enclosures typical of acrylic fixtures. This model is a three-piece sectional tub-shower designed for the tight confines of a bathroom remodel.

# Molded Acrylic Is a Higher-Priced Alternative

For a good idea of how a molded-acrylic tub-shower is made, round up a gang of 6-year-olds and give them each a paper cup. Within five minutes, one of them is bound to put a cup over his mouth and start sucking out the air. Eventually, the cup collapses. This is essentially how you make an acrylic tub-shower. This shell is reinforced with chopped fiberglass and resin, just like a Gelcoat fixture.

Acrylic tub-showers typically cost between two and two-and-a-half times as much as comparable Gelcoat models. Manufacturers say acrylic is more durable, more scratch resistant, easier to maintain, and easier to repair than Gelcoat. Because the shell is formed from a sheet of material far thicker than Gelcoat, the color coat is that much thicker.

Part of the higher expense of acrylic fixtures is explained by the manufacturing process (an elaborate aluminum mold can easily cost $100,000) and partly because more materials are used. One distinguishing

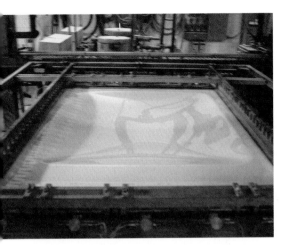

Acrylic tub-showers are vacuum-formed. A ⅛-in.-thick sheet of acrylic plastic is warmed in a 400°F oven and then rolled over the mouth of an aluminum vacuum mold at a Lasco plant in Virginia.

A tub shower in less than a minute. Warm and pliable, the acrylic quickly takes the shape of its mold under the pressure of a vacuum.

After cooling, the finished shell emerges.

feature of an acrylic tub-shower is its dome or ceiling. Because the fixture is formed in a vacuum mold, it must be closed on all sides (manufacturers that offer open-top acrylic tub-shower units form them the same way, but then cut off the dome). Extra material means extra height: Acrylic fixtures typically run to about 84 in. high, several inches taller than a Gelcoat tub-shower.

Although acrylic fixtures get the same fiberglass reinforcement as Gelcoat tub-showers, some resin additives may be a bit different. Lasco®, for instance, adds what it calls microspheres (little balloons) to the resin used in acrylic models to increase rigidity and to make the fixture more resistant to impact damage. Additives also add to the price.

## Building Inspectors May Require a Certified Tub

Once every couple of months, an inspector from the National Association of Home Builders' Research Center walks unannounced into a bathtub factory and chooses a fixture at random. It is pulled off the line and shipped back to the center's lab in Upper Marlboro, Maryland, where Chuck Arnold is waiting to go to work. In rough terms, Arnold's job is to make the plumbing fixture think it has been installed by a careless plumber in a household of overweight, hyperactive chain smokers.

The Research Center is one of a number of independent certifying labs around the country that make sure Gelcoat and acrylic plumbing fixtures meet requirements of the American National Standards Institute. Developed during the 1960s, the ANSI Z-124 performance standard is meant to reassure building officials, builders, and homeowners that plastic tub-showers will perform the way manufacturers claim they will. According to Arnold, building officials in many parts of the country are becoming more

*Check to make sure the tub-shower you have in mind meets local codes—before you have it entombed in the second-floor framing.*

## Installation Tips for Plastic Tub-Showers

Rex Cauldwell, a Virginia plumber and electrician, thought it would be a good idea to support the floor of his new plastic tub so that it wouldn't flex when he used it. Some manufacturers recommend the practice, suggesting the tub floor be bedded in mortar or gypsum plaster. But Cauldwell was intrigued with the possibilities presented by expanding polyurethane foam. So he foamed up the bottom of the tub and set it in place. After the foam had hardened, the tub was as unyielding as a concrete pier, just as Cauldwell had hoped. The foam, however, had hoisted the tub off the floor by more than ¼ in. as it expanded and cured. It required some artful work with a handsaw to settle it back down.

How much urethane foam is too much is one of many lessons Cauldwell has learned in years of installing Gelcoat and acrylic tub-showers. The hardest part of the job is working around the plumbing—maneuvering the fixture past the protruding valve stem and shower arm and attaching it to the waste and overflow line. An excellent explanation of the process is contained in *Installing & Repairing Plumbing Fixtures* (The Taunton Press, 1994) by Peter Hemp, a California plumber. Hemp has a number of suggestions for this tricky piece of business but warns that you should plan on sliding the fixture in and out several times before you get it right.

Tips from Hemp and Cauldwell include the following:

- Make sure the alcove for the tub-shower is framed correctly, with a level floor and plumb walls. Schematic drawings from the manufacturers can be wrong, Hemp says, so the safest route is to have the fixture on site before framing the alcove.
- If possible, install the finish floor first and run it into the tub alcove to eliminate a seam, and potential leak, at the junction of tub and floor.
- If the framed alcove is just a little snug, don't try kicking in a plastic tub-shower the last ½ in. It will crack. Make sure nailing flanges meet framing materials evenly. If they don't, shim between the flange and the framing. Screw holes for the flanges should be predrilled and countersunk.
- A flexible 90-degree elbow on the drain line may help to prevent leaks caused by constant flexing in the floor of the tub, especially if you don't set the tub on mortar, plaster, or foam.
- Consider stuffing fiberglass insulation around tub walls before installation to improve heat retention.

likely to require that new plumbing fixtures meet the Z-124 standard. Small manufacturers that distribute fixtures in limited geographic areas may not go to the trouble or expense of hiring a certifying lab to check quality, but big companies do.

Z-124 simulates what a tub-shower would go through in its lifetime. And what a lifetime. Load tests include lowering a 300-lb. weight into the tub and measuring sag, or applying a 25-lb. force against the shower walls to see how much they bend. Arnold and his colleagues drop a ½-lb. steel ball into the tub to see what happens, burn the fixture with a plumber's torch, heap common chemicals on the surface to see how it will stain, and leave burning cigarettes on the plastic surface to measure damage. Lab technicians even have something called a "xenon weatherometer," a device that compresses five years of window-light exposure into 200 hours. If a tub-shower meets the standards, that fact will be noted on the label or in the literature that comes with the fixture.

Common problems include thin or improperly applied Gelcoat layers that show up in wear and durability tests, and insufficient fiberglass chop around drain-fitting areas and on walls. Acrylic fixtures, Arnold says, do show a more consistent surface finish and fare better in boiling-water and wear-and-cleanability tests. They can, however, suffer from the same structural problems as Gelcoat fixtures. If made correctly, Arnold says, Gelcoat tub-showers seem to perform about as well as the more expensive acrylic models in many of the center's tests.

In addition, the building department in your area may require that a tub-shower meet other fire or building codes. Just because you can buy a tub-shower locally doesn't mean it will get the okay from a by-the-book plumbing inspector in your town. To be safe, check to make sure the tub-shower you have in mind meets local codes—before you have it entombed in the second-floor framing.

# Choose the Right Plastic Tub-Shower

How much you spend makes a big difference in what you get. You can buy an economy-grade Gelcoat fixture for a whole lot less than what you'd spend on a cast-iron tub and tile—$200, say, as opposed to $1,000 and up (prices vary by region). But the Gelcoat will look and feel a lot less substantial. The plastic surface will be more susceptible to damage. A budget model with low shower walls will force you to mount the shower arm in the drywall above the plastic, unless you don't mind stooping to wash your hair. Color choices are limited. These factors suggest that a budget Gelcoat fixture is good for a seasonal home or a children's bathroom.

A more expensive Gelcoat fixture, something that costs $400 or so, will get you higher shower walls, a bigger tub, and a wider choice of colors, all of which are attractive features for not a lot more money. But at the top of the pecking order are acrylic tub-showers. Although they cost a couple of hundred dollars more, starting at about $750, acrylic fixtures have some inherent advantages over Gelcoat. As one manufacturer put it, you get a better material and more of it—a harder and thicker shell that does better in the NAHB Research Center's cleaning and wear tests. Its domed roof simplifies bathroom construction and allows you to add a steam generator to the shower if you want. With their undulating contours, acrylic tub-showers are sleek and stylish in a way that basic tile isn't. But here's the rub: An acrylic fixture at the upper end of the price range approaches the cost of a cast-iron tub and tile shower walls.

There are a half-dozen or so major players in the market and scores of smaller companies. If you're considering a plastic fixture, it's probably worth your time to visit a well-stocked plumbing-supply house and compare brands. Whether you choose acrylic or Gelcoat, look for heft and weight as well as attractive styling and a blemish-free finish.

No matter what you end up with, remember that the enemy of plastic fixtures is improper cleaning: the compulsive germophobe armed with a can of Comet® and a scouring pad. If you buy plastic, make sure you use only the cleaners recommended by the manufacturer.

*Price estimates noted are from 1998.

---

**Scott Gibson** *is a contributing editor for* Fine Homebuilding.

## Sources

**Aqua Glass Corp.**
320 Industrial Park Rd.
P.O. Box 412
Adamsville, TN 38310
(731) 632-0911
www.aquaglass.com

**Lasco Bathware**
3255 E. Miraloma Ave.
Anaheim, CA 02806
(800) 877-0464
www.lascobathware.com

**Luxury Bath Systems**
1958 Brandon Ct.
Glendale Heights,
IL 60139
(800) 822-7905
www.luxurybaths.com

# Installing a Leakproof Shower Pan

■ BY TOM MEEHAN

In the past 10 years, I have installed well over a thousand shower pans. Of all those pans, only two have leaked. One pan belonged to my father-in-law, and the other belonged to my dentist. My father-in-law is a conservative man who likes to have all his ducks in a row. My dentist was well aware that I had two root canals coming up in the near future. Needless to say, I made sure that fixing these two jobs was at the top of my list.

After a lot of work, I found that faulty drain-assembly fittings were responsible for the leaks in both cases (honest). In the process of rebuilding the pans, I discovered a simple test that would have saved me all that misery. But more on that later; first, let's start building the pan.

**After the membrane is installed,** the author plugs the drain and pours gallons of water into the shower. Better to find leaks now than after the tile is in.

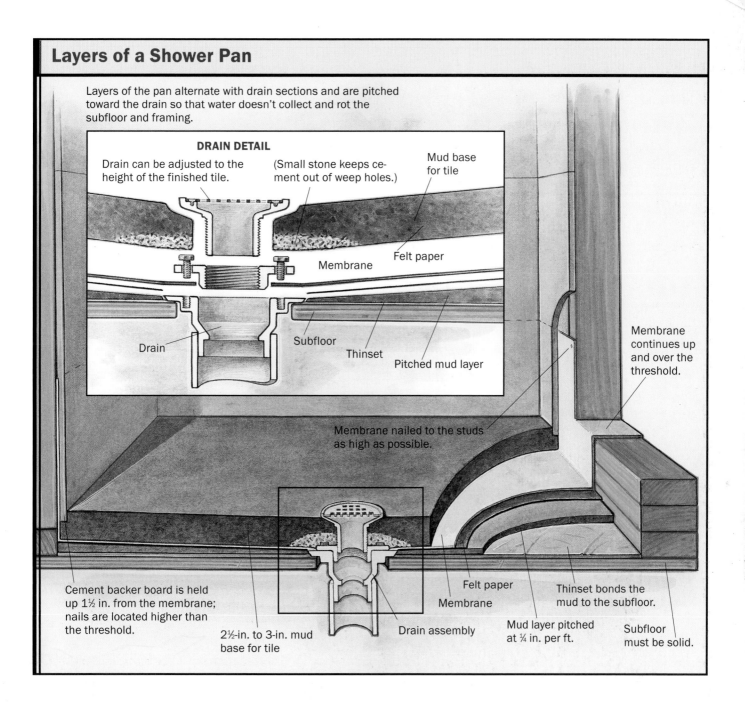

## Layers of a Shower Pan

Layers of the pan alternate with drain sections and are pitched toward the drain so that water doesn't collect and rot the subfloor and framing.

**DRAIN DETAIL**

Drain can be adjusted to the height of the finished tile.

(Small stone keeps cement out of weep holes.)

Mud base for tile

Felt paper

Membrane

Drain

Subfloor

Thinset

Pitched mud layer

Membrane continues up and over the threshold.

Membrane nailed to the studs as high as possible.

Cement backer board is held up 1½ in. from the membrane; nails are located higher than the threshold.

2½-in. to 3-in. mud base for tile

Drain assembly

Felt paper

Membrane

Mud layer pitched at ¼ in. per ft.

Thinset bonds the mud to the subfloor.

Subfloor must be solid.

# Pitch the Floor under the Membrane

Before I install the pan, I clean the subfloor in the shower area thoroughly. I look for anything that might punch or wear a hole in the membrane in the future. I set any nail heads in the lower 6–8 in. of the framing, and I put an extra flap of membrane over any nail plate installed to protect the plumbing.

When I'm building a shower pan, my first concern is that the subfloor is structurally sound. If it's not, I add a layer of ½-in. plywood before the plumber sets the drain assembly. I also do an extra step that I think makes a huge improvement over a standard installation. I like to pitch the shower floor to the drain area before I put the membrane material down (drawing above). A pitched mud base allows any water that may reach the membrane to

After the subfloor has been swept clean, a layer of latex-modified thinset is applied to bond the layer of mud that follows.

To build up the pitch on the pan floor, a fairly dry mix of 1 part portland cement to 3 or 4 parts sand is used to form the mud base. The mix should be just wet enough to form clumps when squeezed.

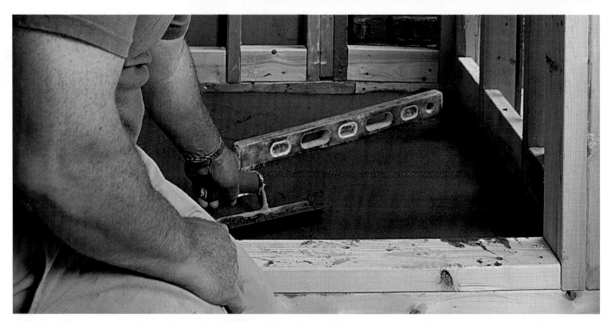

Using a 2-ft. level as a gauge, the author floats a pitch of about ¼ in. per ft. from the pan's perimeter to the drain.

drain through the weep holes in the drain assembly.

To create this pitch, I float a layer of mud over the shower floor. The mud, a mixture of 1 part portland cement to 3 or 4 parts sand, is just wet enough that it holds together if you grab a handful. To bond the mud layer to the plywood subfloor, I first apply a layer of latex-modified thinset to the subfloor (top left photo, facing page).

The mud mix is spread on top of the thinset, leaving a pitch of ¼ in. per ft. from the outside perimeter of the shower to the drain (right and bottom photos, facing page). I pack the mud with a wooden float and smooth it with a flat steel trowel. This mud layer dries overnight.

The next day, I cover the mud with a layer of 15-lb. felt paper, cutting the paper tightly around the drain. The felt paper protects the membrane from any mud grit that could abrade it. The felt paper also isolates the finished shower pan from any movement that might occur in the subfloor.

## A Vinyl Membrane Keeps the Water in the Pan

Now I'm ready for the shower-pan membrane. I use a vinyl membrane called Chloraloy®, made by The Noble Company. I usually buy a 4-ft. by 50-ft. roll that costs about $360. The membrane is also sold by the piece; a 4-ft. by 6-ft. section costs about $50.

I roll out the membrane on a clean floor and map out the pan with a felt-tip pen (photo right). First, I draw the four sides of the shower pan (my fold lines) and then add 7 in. to each side for the cutlines. The fold lines let me position the membrane in the shower without having to shift it around a lot. Measuring and mapping the pan also help me to avoid mistakes in my calculations. I always double-check the lines before cutting.

**The membrane is rolled out on a clean floor,** and the outer perimeter of the shower pan is drawn with a felt-tip pen and labeled as fold lines. An extra 7 in. is added in each direction, and the membrane is cut to those lines.

Once the membrane is centered in the shower, the excess is carefully folded into the corners.

A roofing nail secures the fold to the framing. As the rest of the perimeter is tacked to the studs, the membrane should not be stretched too tightly.

# Folded Corners Let the Membrane Lie Flat

Before I move the membrane, I take off the top plastic ring of the drain assembly and put it aside until later. The bolts are left threaded into the lower drain assembly. I then drop the membrane into place, pushing all the fold lines to their proper outside edges.

In the corners where excess membrane bunches up, I push the liner directly into the corner with my finger. The excess corner material is then folded into a pleat so that it lies against the framing as flat as possible (photo above). Keeping the folds flat prevents bulges in the backer board applied over the membrane.

I secure the fold to the framing with one roofing nail along the top edge (photo below). As I move toward the next corner, I nail the upper edge of the liner at each stud, always keeping the liner square to the wall and taking care not to pull it off the floor or to stretch it too tight.

One of the most crucial steps is cutting and connecting the membrane to the plastic drain assembly (sidebar, facing page.) First, I mark the heads of the four drain-assembly bolts where they touch the membrane. Then, with a fresh blade in my utility knife, I make a small slit for each bolt and push the membrane down over the bolts. Next, I cut from bolt to bolt in a circle, following the inside of the drain. Cuts should always be made toward the inside of the drain to avoid slipping with the knife and cutting the floor area of the membrane.

Before I install the top ring of the drain assembly, I lift the liner around the drain and make sure the bottom plastic ring is clear of dirt or grit. I like to adhere the underside of the membrane to the top of the drain-assembly plate with PVC membrane cement or an elastomeric sealant. After applying the cement to both the membrane's underside and the top of the baseplate, I quickly press them together, place

## Cut Carefully to Connect the Drain

The drain must be assembled so that it forms a watertight seal with the membrane, so membrane cuts must be precise. First, bolt heads are marked. Next, small cuts are made to expose just the heads. Following the inside of the drain, a circular cut is made between bolt heads. After the membrane is cut, membrane adhesive or sealant is applied to the underside of the membrane. The top part of the drain is then slid into place and cemented, and bolts are tightened slowly and evenly.

Mark the bolt locations.

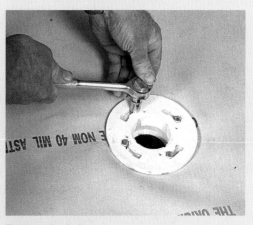

Cut in a circle between the bolts.

Apply the adhesive.

Tighten the bolts.

the top ring in position, and slowly tighten the bolts, applying equal pressure on each bolt. At the threshold, I cut the membrane along the framed opening, fold it over, and nail it to the threshold framing. To avoid leaks at the cut corners, I fold and glue additional pieces of membrane into the corners with PVC cement.

To test the pan, I first insert an expandable rubber drain plug into the lower part of the drain and tighten it with a wrench. I then dump enough water to cover the entire shower pan 2 in. to 3 in. deep, and I let the pan sit overnight. The next day, I make sure the level of the water hasn't gone down and then check for leaks in the ceiling directly below the shower stall.

I try to make it a point to have the builder or homeowner witness the shower-

**TIP**

*Round over the corners of the steel trowel. A square corner could slice or puncture the membrane if you're not careful.*

stall test. Once the pan has passed inspection, I make sure that no one steps into the shower pan until I have poured the mud base for the tile.

## Keep the Backer Board Off the Shower Floor

All the shower stalls that I tile now have cement backer board under the wall tile. The bottom course of backer board is installed over the membrane, but I always try to install the upper sheets and the ceiling before the pan goes in to keep big clunky feet like mine off the delicate membrane.

After the pan has been installed and tested, I put a protective layer of felt paper over the membrane while I hang the bottom pieces of backer board. All the backer board is attached to the studs with either 1½-in. galvanized roofing nails or galvanized screws. I make sure that the bottom pieces are at least 2 ft. wide to provide adequate strength for spanning the stud bays.

When installing the bottom course of backer board, I keep in mind two important

rules. First, I keep the board 1½ in. from the pan floor. If the backer board is installed too low, moisture can wick up into the wall, creating a variety of problems. The second rule is never to nail the board lower than the top of the threshold or the step into the shower. Nailing 4 in. from the finished floor usually works well. If the drain ever clogs, low nailing could cause a leak.

## Thick Mud Makes a Sturdy Tile Base

I'm now ready to put the mud layer on top of the membrane. For this layer, I use a 4:1 mixture (sand-to-portland cement). I pour a couple of handfuls of ¼-in. stone around the base of the drain to help keep the weep holes in the drain assembly free and clear of cement (photo below).

Again, I mix the cement to a consistency that forms a ball when compressed in my hand (top left photo, facing page). When I'm satisfied with the mix, I dump a good amount into the pan. The weight of the mix keeps the membrane from creeping. With

**A couple of handfuls of pea stone keep the mud mix from clogging the weep holes in the drain.**

The mud for the shower floor should be just wet enough to stay in a clump when squeezed in the hand.

A 2-ft. level is used to make sure that the shower floor is flat and evenly pitched to the drain. The level also doubles as a tool for screeding the mud.

this shower stall, I packed the cement about 2 in. to 3 in. thick to maintain the ¼-in.-per-ft. pitch from the wall to the drain that had already been established.

I used a 2-ft. level to straighten the perimeter of the mud layer. It's a good idea for beginners to establish a level line around the pan first. Again, I use a wooden float to pack the mud. A straightedge, in this case my 2-ft. level, and a flat steel trowel let me pitch the mud smoothly and evenly to the drain (photo above right). The upper portion of the drain can be adjusted so that it will be flush with the installed tile. One precaution I take is to round over the corners of the steel trowel (photo right). A square corner could slice or puncture the membrane if I'm not careful. I keep working the surface to eliminate any voids or low spots in the mud that can collect water once the tile is installed. When the mud layer is smooth, evenly pitched, and level around the perimeter, I let it sit overnight, and then I'm ready to install the tile in the morning.

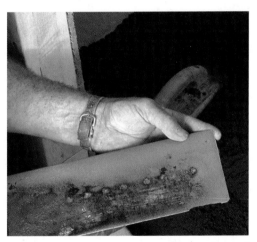

The author rounds the corners of his steel trowel so that there are no sharp corners to puncture the membrane while he's working the mud layer.

*Tom Meehan is a second-generation tile installer and owner of The Cape Cod Tileworks, a tile store in Harwich, Massachusetts.*

# A Walk Through Shower Doors

■ BY ANDY ENGEL

In our first house, my wife and I lived with a cheap sliding door on the bathtub for far longer than I care to admit. The twin channels of its cheesy aluminum track collected soap scum in their inaccessible crevices. Attempting to plug the leaks where the track met the tub-surround, a previous owner had smeared silicone caulk inside the corners. Water ignored the caulk, however, while mildew just plain loved it.

Then there were the rollers from which the door hung. They derailed regularly, trapping the occupant in the shower. And because the doors had no handle on the shower side, getting one back on track from inside the tub was a challenge.

When I remodeled that bathroom, some enterprising neighbor scavenged the doors and their tracks from curbside before the garbage truck came. Even at that price, though, the new owner got no bargain.

## Sliding-Door Tracks Can Now Be Cleaned Easily

Sliding doors have come a long way since I left mine on the curb. For one thing, the twin-trench tracks are, for the most part,

history. They've been replaced by bottom tracks that slope with one easy-to-clean plane into the shower or tub. To guide the door bottoms, most manufacturers provide a small replaceable plastic block in the center of the bottom track. Two channels that are milled in the block steer the doors.

Our old rollers hung from cheap, die-cast flanges that had cracked. Most manufacturers today use more durable stainless-steel flanges and sealed ball-bearing rollers. I wouldn't bother buying a slider that could not make these claims. Another minimum standard that I would look for is stainless-steel screws everywhere.

The top tracks, side jambs, and door-frames seem to have improved as well. Today, except on low-end doors, the aluminum used for tracks and frames is protected by anodization. Anodization is a process whereby an aluminum surface is electrolytically coated with aluminum oxide, a nonreactive substance that's second only to the diamond in its hardness.

The best aluminum tracks and frames are polished before anodization to remove marks left by the extrusion process. Prior to anodization, aluminum can be treated or dyed to resemble pewter, stainless steel, copper, brushed bronze, or polished brass. At

**Frameless shower enclosures** offer a clean design and can make a bathroom look larger.

## Slider Tracks Have Come a Long Way

Unlike yesterday's enclosed, trenchlike tracks, new sloped bottom tracks are easily cleaned. Most have a plastic block in the center that guides the doors. Removing this block allows full access to the bottoms of the glass panels.

least one company, Basco®, has finishes that closely match the finish colors offered by major plumbing-fixture manufacturers.

Powder coating is another common finish for extruded aluminum. Powder coating is done by electrically charging the aluminum extrusion so that dry pigments stick to it. The coated aluminum is then baked at around 400°F, fusing the pigments into a durable, colorful finish.

Brass is one more, albeit expensive, option for track and frames. The chief advantage of brass is that it can be plated with the actual metals that aluminum can only mimic. I was struck by how closely the chrome finish on one brass frame resembled the lovingly polished bumper of a '57 Chevy® I'd seen at a recent car show.

Tom Whittaker of Mr. Shower Door® in Norwalk, Connecticut, told me that he has brass frames plated after they're cut to length instead of buying preplated stock. That way, cut ends are plated as well, which minimizes chances that the plating will peel.

A quick word about caulking framed doors. Although the temptation to avoid the look of caulk on the outside of the

### How Best to Clean Shower Enclosures

If you have Web access and care about your bath enclosure, go to www.glasswebsite.com/bema/cleaning.html. You'll find the results of a study sponsored by The Bath Enclosure Manufacturers' Association on the cleaning power of major brands of bathroom cleansers, as well as their effect on aluminum.

The short story: Do not use vinegar-based cleaners, abrasive powders, or steel or Teflon® pads. The favored cleanser is Comet Non-Abrasive Bathroom Cleaner.

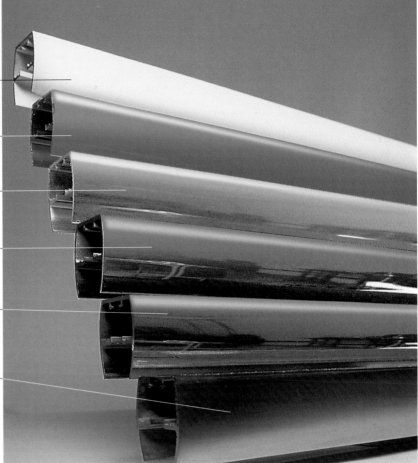

Powder-coated aluminum

Gold-anodized aluminum

Chrome-anodized aluminum

Chrome-plated brass

Nickel-plated brass

Brushed-nickel-plated brass

**Slider tracks are aluminum or brass. Anodized aluminum mimics a variety of finishes, while plated brass offers the real thing.**

frame can be strong, you should resist it. Caulking the outside of the frame forces water back into the tub. If you caulk the inside, water that gets past the caulk will drip onto the floor.

## Are Glass Shower Doors Dangerous?

Every day, millions of us stand naked in a small glass enclosure, eyes closed against an irritant that drips down our foreheads. We call this seeming mass irrational behavior washing our hair in the shower. We do this task without a second thought because of an unarticulated confidence that the glass of our shower enclosures won't easily break.

Building codes specify safety glazing in bath areas. This product can be plastic; laminated glass, which has a tough plastic sheet embedded between layers of glass; or tempered glass. Plastic doors scratch and are found only in the cheapest units. Of the two

types of glass, tempered is by far the most common, mainly because of cost. Also, laminated glass is somewhat more prone to cracking. (This issue isn't a safety concern, however, because the plastic sheet keeps big artery-slicing glass shards from falling out.)

Tempered glass is four times stronger than the same thickness of regular window glass. Bill Furr of Coastal Industries®, a shower-enclosure manufacturer in Jacksonville, Florida, told me that he's demonstrated the strength of tempered glass by standing on the center of a standard shower-door panel whose ends are supported on 6-in. blocks. The glass simply bows to the floor.

Tempering begins in a furnace that heats the glass to nearly melting. The glass is then quickly chilled with cold air. This sudden cooling shrinks the outside of the glass, tensioning the skin and compressing the core.

You can break a sheet of tempered glass by relieving the skin tension. Scratching an edge or drilling a hole does just that and

A three-panel slider offers greater tub access. This feature is particularly useful for parents who are bathing toddlers, or for someone looking for elbowroom to stretch out in the bath.

A shower screen is great for bathing small children, but splashing while showering can be trouble.

turns a sheet of tempered glass into a pile of small pieces, as you may have seen on the street in the aftermath of an auto accident. The idea is that small pieces are less likely to inflict dangerous wounds.

By law, tempered glass has to be permanently marked as such. So look for a small tempering seal, or bug, etched in a corner of every panel that goes into your bath.

## Hinged Screens Provide Access to All of the Bathtub

Although sliders are common, they aren't perfect. At best, most sliding doors on bathtubs access only half the tub, a disadvantage for parents bathing young children. Preventing a soaped-up toddler from slipping below the surface is tough enough with full tub access. Basco makes a triple-panel slider that allows access to two-thirds of a tub, but it has a lower track. Although less imperative than lifeguarding, leaning one's forearms on the lower track for balance while scrubbing down a toddler is painful. Curtains have no lower track.

Still, curtains may not restrict shower water to the tub as well as an enclosure might. For example, my own kids are now of an age where they resent parental supervision in the shower, but they aren't yet old enough to be relied on to close the shower curtain fully.

One solution to this dilemma is a shower screen. Popular in Europe, shower screens have no track and cover about two-thirds of a 5-ft.-long tub. Screens can be a single panel that swings out to provide tub access, but if you go this route, be sure that there is enough clearance so that the door doesn't hit, for example, the toilet. For tighter quarters, many manufacturers produce folding screens that take up half the space of a single panel. With either type, a sweep seals the door bottom to the tub.

Tom Whittaker recommends that his customers first go home and shower with a curtain that's only two-thirds closed to see if they can live with the overspray. According to Whittaker, screens work best with showerheads that point straight down and spray gently, thereby minimizing splashing.

John Veras told me that his company, Duschqueen in Wykoff, New Jersey, supplies a stationary panel that covers 1 ft. or so of the plumbed end of a tub. A single or folding screen hinges from the other end of the tub and seals to the stationary panel. This configuration solves the problem of a partially open shower while closing off considerably less of the tub from parents.

Unless the shower's user squeegees all the water from the glass before exiting, some is bound to drip onto the bathroom floor, as is the case with any out-swing door. Single-panel out-swing doors can have a gutter applied to their bottom that directs water back into the tub. That's not done with folding doors, however, because such a gutter would interfere with fully folding the panels. And if you want a frameless look, even a gutter of clear plastic can be a visual distraction.

Stall-shower doors are generally out-swing. The building code requires this style of door in many jurisdictions to facilitate rescue should a bather collapse in the shower. Some stall-shower doors have a pivot about one-third of the door width in from the edge so that they open partially into the shower. Check with your local building official before installing this space-saving door style.

Magnetic seals have become common on stall doors. They are watertight, but they frequently come in dark colors that show off soap scum. As with any door, open and close the display model of a stall door several times before buying. Any troubles a door displays in a showroom will worsen with use.

## A Checklist of Shower-Door Dos and Don'ts

- Even the best door seals will leak when the curb slopes away from the shower.
- Shower doors often weigh upward of 80 lb. Don't forget to put sturdy blocking inside the wall for hinge screws.
- Shower-door handles are not grab bars. Mount any grab bars securely to the wall.
- It is a code violation to swing a shower door inward. Plan the shower so that your out-swing door doesn't hit, say, the toilet or the towel bar. And remember, a towel bar mounted on the door requires just as much clearance as one mounted on the wall.
- Tempered glass can't be scribe-fitted. Stone kneewall caps or decorative tile that protrudes from the wall can look great, but fitting a glass panel or trying to seal a door to them is likely to give your enclosure contractor fits. Try to design walls that intersect glass to be flat and plumb.
- Says Tom Whittaker of Mr. Shower Door, "Pointing your showerhead at the enclosure door is dumb." Aim your showerhead at a wall, the floor, a stationary glass panel or some other spot less likely to leak than the door.
- The sheer volume of water pumped from multihead so-called body sprays can overwhelm even the best shower-door seals. A high curb on the shower and a floor drain in the bathroom can avoid disaster if your shower includes a body spray.

# Frameless Doors Open Views and Create a Potential Problem

Frameless shower enclosures are what's hot right now (photo p. 63). Furthering this clean look, clear glass has overtaken obscure glass in popularity. A frameless enclosure with clear glass can make a bathroom look bigger or show off a beautifully tiled shower.

Although clear glass looks great in magazines, remember that keeping it clear takes diligent cleaning. Water spots don't show as quickly on obscure glass.

One reason to frame a door is that the frame protects the edge of the tempered-glass panel. Barry Miller related this story on *Fine Homebuilding*'s on-line discussion board, "Breaktime": "I was replacing one frameless door after cleaning the tracks—(I) can't do it properly with doors in place—and I ticked a corner of the door on the tub. All of a sudden, I was holding air and had a pile of glass pebbles all around my feet." The "tick" to the edge of Miller's door relieved the tempered panel's surface tension, causing the glass to shatter.

Miller's story isn't enough to put me off frameless doors entirely, but it does beg the question: Can the track be cleaned easily without removing the doors? I would closely examine the unit in the showroom to be certain before I bought a slider.

Of course, frameless shower-enclosure manufacturers take measures to help ensure that their customers don't share Miller's experience. For example, unobtrusive foam bumpers cushion the vulnerable edge of door panels where they close against a wall or another panel. Clearly, these bumpers bear watching. If they show wear, replace them.

Frames offer one more advantage, which may benefit the manufacturer more than the consumer. A thin glass panel or door feels flimsy, although it may be perfectly safe. Adding a frame stiffens the glass at small cost to the manufacturer.

The most common glass thickness in less expensive framed doors is $\frac{5}{32}$ in. Frameless panels are at least $\frac{1}{4}$-in. glass and more likely to be $\frac{3}{8}$ in. Glass as thick as $\frac{1}{2}$ in. is common in frameless doors, and doors made of it feel massive. If you want the feel of $\frac{1}{2}$-in. glass, make sure your supplier's hinges or rollers are rated for the weight.

# Glass Must Be Cut Before Tempering

The bread and butter of shower-enclosure manufacturers is stock units that fit a standard 5-ft. tub or shower opening. That's because manufacturers can order the frames, and particularly the tempered glass, in quantity. As a consequence, stock-size enclosures are markedly less expensive than custom ones. I can buy a standard 5-ft. framed slider for $150 or so and a frameless 5-ft. slider for about $400. A custom hinged door half that width will set me back at least $800. And like anything custom, you can buy as fancy a shower enclosure as your mortgage will allow.

The measurements for custom shower enclosures must be precise because the installer can't take a little off the top to make an imperfectly sized tempered-glass panel fit well. All the custom-enclosure installers with whom I spoke will measure a job only after all the tile or stone is installed. However, they crave involvement in the design stage, hoping to avoid the need to work around prior errors.

# What to Look for in a Frameless Enclosure

People who want frameless shower doors usually want to minimize distracting hardware. Some hardware is unavoidable, though, such as hinges or top and bottom tracks for a sliding door. About the only way to minimize the visual impact of a slider's track is to use a thin-profile brass track. More hardware options exist for hinged doors and stationary panels, however. There are three main styles of hinges: wall mount, pivoting, and glass to glass.

Wall-mount hinges are almost self-explanatory (sidebar, right). One side screws into the wall, and the other affixes to the glass door, either by clamping or by means of a bolt through a hole drilled in the glass prior to its tempering. In either case, to provide room for the body of the hinge, the glass of the door is notched to the hinge supplier's specifications, which also happens prior to tempering.

Wall-mount hinges typically offer ⅛ in. or less of adjustability. They can be shimmed slightly away from the wall to make up for a minor out-of-plumb condition, but it's critical that the wall be straight.

If your wall is seriously out of plumb, hinging the door from a stationary panel may solve your problem. Mounting tracks for stationary panels come in a variety of depths and can hide the variation between a plumb panel and a not-so-plumb wall. Most suppliers told me that stationary panels must be at least 4 in. wide, and unless they also affix to the ceiling, a metal header should be used to brace the top of any stationary panel.

Glass-to-glass hinges affix to both the door and the panel in the same way that wall-mount hinges affix to the door. Both types allow an uninterrupted bottom seal on the door, an advantage in this most-likely-to-leak spot.

## A Sampling of Shower-Door Hinges

**Wall-mount hinges.** They are simple to use when the mounting wall is plumb. Solid blocking for hinge screws is crucial.

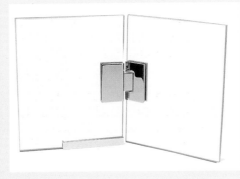

**Glass-to-glass hinges.** When the mounting wall is out of plumb, hanging the door from a plumb stationary panel can work.

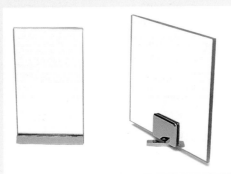

**Pivot hinges.** Mounted top and bottom, pivot hinges offer the least obtrusion into a clear-glass enclosure.

## Mounting Options for Stationary Panels

**Aluminum channel.** Deeper channels can hide the difference between an out-of-plumb wall and a plumb panel.

**Wall-mount clamps.** Clamps provide an unframed look but require the panel to be notched or drilled.

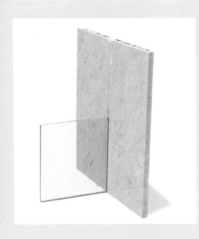

**Dado mount.** Dadoes are hardware-free but require exacting measurements and sure waterproofing.

Pivoting hinges mount to the floor and either the ceiling, the upper track or the upper stationary panel (sidebar, above). Many people believe that these hinges offer the least obtrusive look. By moving the pivots in from the edge of the door by several inches, it's often possible to gain the clearance that's necessary for, say, a towel bar to be placed on an adjacent wall.

## Panels Mount to the Wall with Track, Clamps, or Dadoes

There are three common methods of mounting panels to walls. The most common is a U-shaped track (sidebar, left). Stainless-steel screws through the back of the track (and into solid blocking) hold it in place. The glass slips into the U and then is sealed to the track with silicone caulk. The best silicone caulk is called water-clear or aquarium sealant. It's almost invisible when dry and costs about $30 per tube from C. R. Laurence Co.

Tracks mount glass securely and are easily sealed to the wall. However, they frame the glass, a look that many wish to avoid. Mounting the glass with clamps may be less obtrusive. Clamps affix to the glass much like hinges, with notches and bolt holes. Water-clear silicone caulk then seals the panels to the wall.

The least obtrusive look comes from mounting the glass in a channel in the tile or stone. But many installers shy away from these installations. If the channel is created by leaving a gap in the tile or stone that goes all the way to the substrate, enclosure installers worry about hidden leaks. An alternative when using stone is to dado a channel into the slabs. Because this dado doesn't extend to the substrate, it's no more likely to leak than is the rest of the stone.

Don't plan to enclose more than two sides of a glass panel in a dado, however. Imagine the likelihood of scratching an edge and exploding the tempered glass while trying to maneuver the top, bottom and edge of a panel into a dado.

## Clear-Plastic Door Seals for a Frameless Enclosure

Some people think that even the clearest door seals interfere with the clean look of a frameless enclosure. One solution is not to bother with any seals at all and to build your entire bathroom floor like a custom shower base, with a waterproofing membrane and a central floor drain. Of course, if you did this, you might not need a shower enclosure in the first place.

Short of having an all-shower bathroom, you can get effective door seals of clear polycarbonate or vinyl that, along with good planning of your showerhead's field of fire, will keep the floor dry. Vinyl is best for seals that must be flexible, such as door-bottom sweeps. Polycarbonate is stiffer and is generally used for seals that don't bend much, such as the handle-side seal on a hinged door.

The sleekest looking handle-side door seal that I saw was achieved by mating chamfered edges on the door and the stationary panel. Foam tape covered the chamfered edge of the panel to cushion the door's closing. Because this type of edge seal essentially reduces the tolerance on the handle side of the door to zero, chamfered-edge seals call for an experienced installer.

One particular problem occurs if you want a sliding door in a shower that has a spray head at each end. If both heads are in use, some water is bound to sneak between the doors. A sliding door designed for a

steam shower would solve this problem. Steam doors are sealed on all edges, and many major manufacturers make them.

I've come to like the look of clear-glass shower enclosures. Now I plan to install one in our still-incomplete master bath. That we'll enjoy its look justifies the cost of a moderately priced enclosure. In the kids' bathroom, though, we'll keep the curtain. I'm sure they'll eventually learn to close it.

*Price estimates noted are from 2001.

*Andy Engel* is executive editor at Fine Homebuilding.

## Sources

**Basco**
7201 Snider Rd.
Mason, OH 45040
(800) 543-1938
www.bascoshower-door.com

**Coastal Industries**
P.O. 16091
Jacksonville, FL 32245
(800) 874-8601
www.coastalind.com

**C. R. Laurence Co.**
P.O. Box 25893
Los Angeles, CA 90058
(800) 421-6144
www.crlaurence.com

**Duschqueen**
461 W. Main St.
Wyckoff, NJ 07481
(800) 348-8080
www.duschqueeninc.com

**Mr. Shower Door**
651 Connecticut Ave.
Norwalk, CT 06854
(800) 633-3667
www.mrshowerdoor.com

# Residential Steam Showers

▪ BY ANDY ENGEL

There was a Finn, the only Finn, who would not take a sauna. "It isn't that I can't," he said, "I simply do not wanna." So begins my favorite Garrison Keillor poem, which I quote for two reasons:

- Although a steam shower differs from a sauna by virtue of its higher humidity, they have a common purpose: fostering relaxation.
- For a lot of people who are building a new home or remodeling an old one, the reason not to have a steam shower won't be that they can't, but that they "simply do not wanna."

Adding steam to a shower isn't pricey, at least in the context of building a home. A standard shower can be upgraded to a steam shower for about $2,000. Of course, this amount is a starting point, and there is no limit on what any shower could cost a dedicated spender.

Reactions to bathing in steam vary. Jennifer Black, a bath designer in Woodbury, Connecticut, urges her clients to try a steam shower before installing one. She has learned that some people find being enveloped in steam too claustrophobic. These people can use their money on a vacation once their home is done.

Lane Meehan's reaction to her steam shower is more typical. Lane, co-owner of Cape Cod Tileworks, finds steam showers relaxing and claims that her steam shower was the only sure means of easing her child's croup. Glen Stewart, an Encinitas, California, furnituremaker, typically uses his shower to clear his sinuses. And, perhaps more creatively, he has used his shower to steam warped wood so that he could clamp it flat.

## Steam-Shower Enclosures Differ from Regular Ones

So you've taken a steam shower, and you liked it. Now what? Whether you're building new or renovating, there are a few things you need to know. First and foremost is that shower-enclosure walls and ceilings must be covered entirely with a water-impervious material such as ceramic tile or stone. Painted drywall—even the water-resistant drywall often used above one-piece shower units—is not acceptable.

Another requirement for the shower enclosure is a door designed to keep in the steam. To keep in steam, the door (or a panel above it) must reach to the ceiling, and it must seal to its frame with the indoor equivalent of weatherstripping.

Manufacturers of acrylic or fiberglass steam-shower units supply doors of this type with the unit. If your shower is to have a custom door, the contractor has to know he's supplying a door for a steam shower. In many cases, custom doors include an operable transom to allow moisture to escape when the shower is being used for everyday bathing.

Another important detail is to slope or curve the shower's ceiling. This detail is important because steam condenses. If the shower ceiling is flat, condensed water rains down in a random, cold, unwelcome manner. Condensation on a sloped ceiling, however, follows the ceiling down to the wall instead of dripping on your skin.

**A steam shower is a conventional shower with a steam head.** The chief caveat is that all shower surfaces must be covered with a water-impervious material such as tile. It's also a good idea to slope the ceiling to guide condensation to the wall, not to your shoulders.

**Believe it or not, heat and humidity can be relaxing.** Steam billowing from this fitting can quickly raise the shower's temperature and humidity to points exceeding an August day in New Orleans.

**A door that seals is another necessity.** Run-of-the-mill shower doors are intended to contain only liquid water. To keep in steam, weatherstripping is needed.

**Buy the package.** Several manufacturers supply acrylic shower units set up for steam with an arched ceiling and a sealing door.

## A Tilesetter's Steam-Shower Advice

- **On substrates:** When installing a steam shower, I never use drywall as a substrate or mastic as a bonding agent. Cement backer board and old-fashioned mud jobs will not deteriorate with steam. Bond the stone or tile to the wall substrate with a good latex-modified thinset mortar. When I am installing stone, I skim-coat the back of each piece with thinset mortar to block the pores and to help the stone have a denser composition.

- **On grouting:** Two types of grouts can be used: latex modified and epoxy (epoxy grout cannot be used with limestone). Latex modified is the most common and easiest to work with.

- **On sealing stone and grout:** Always seal a full shower stall with a good impregnator, such as 511 Impregnator from Miracle Sealants Co. A good impregnator can be expensive but is worth every penny. With natural stone, this process should be repeated once at least every two years.

*Tom Meehan is co-owner of Cape Cod Tileworks in Harwich, Massachusetts.*

None of the manufacturers or installers with whom I spoke strongly advocated any special measures, such as a plastic vapor barrier behind the wall and ceiling substrate. All of them, however, recommended a bath fan ducted to the outside, a good practice in any bathroom. That no one recommended a vapor barrier made me nervous at first. But when I learned that most residential steam showers use only 1 gal. or so of water per

**Steam generators can hide in just about any nook or cranny.** While most generators are designed to fit in closets or vanities, this unit by Mr. Steam can also fit between the studs of a standard wall.

## Sources

### STEAM GENERATORS

**Airmist**
P.O. Box 297
Hamel, MN 55340
(800) 728-6226
www.airmist.com
*Tylo generators*

**Amerec**
P.O. Box 2258
Woodinville, WA 98072
(800) 331-0349
www.amerec.com

**Baltic Leisure**
(800) 441-7147
www.balticleisure.com

**Mr. Steam**
43-20 34th St.
Long Island City, NY 11101
(800) 767-8326
www.mrsteam.com

**Steam**
275 Veterans Blvd.
Rutherford, NJ 07070
(201) 933-0700
www.steamist.com

**Steamtec**
84-09 168 St.
Jamaica, NY 11432
(718) 297-7601

**Sven's Sauna**
(800) 750-2944
bygginc.com

### STEAM-SHOWER UNITS

**Jacuzzi**
2121 N. Cal Blvd.
Walnut Creek, CA 94596
(800) 288-4002
www.jacuzzi.com

**Kohler**
444 Highland Dr.
Kohler, WI 53044
(800) 456-4537
www.kohler.com

**Lasco Bathware**
3255 E. Miraloma Ave.
Anaheim, CA 02806
(800) 877-0464
www.lascobath-ware.com

**Maax**
600 Cameron St.
Ste-Marie Beauce
Quebec G6E 1B2
(800) 463-6229
www.maax.com

use, I relaxed. Some of the endless conventional showers taken by teenagers must put twice that amount of vapor into the air.

## Where Does the Steam Come From?

The heart of any steam shower is the steam generator (photo above). Steam generators are typically suitcase-size electric boilers that hide in a vanity, closet, basement, or heated attic near the shower. At least one manufacturer, Mr. Steam®, makes a generator that can fit between the studs of a 2x4 wall. Wherever it's hidden, a steam generator must be accessible for servicing. Also, most manufacturers

recommend that the generator be placed within a 25-ft. pipe run of the shower.

A steam generator needs a water feed, and most need a 220v electrical supply. Steam generators pull between 20 amps and 70 amps (or even more), depending on the size of the enclosure. There is an exception. Mr. Steam makes Steam@home, a 120v steam generator that plugs into a dedicated 20-amp outlet. The unit is designed to heat up only a small, one-person acrylic shower stall.

The generator capacity you need depends primarily on the size of the shower enclosure. Several other factors apply, however. For example, stone absorbs more heat than tile. Having a window, skylight, high ceiling,

> *Most steam showers include a bench. If yours does, the steam head should be well away from the bench to minimize the risk of burns.*

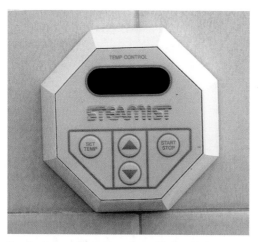

**Controls vary in cost and sophistication. The least-expensive control option is a simple on/off switch on a timer. You can also add a thermostat to maintain a steadily steamy environment.**

facing steam slot space to disperse the steam and takes into account the fact that steam rises. The exception to this rule is if you're combining a steam shower with a bathtub. In this case, the head should be a similar distance above the tub rim. Because these heads get hot, people are less likely to lean on them when the head is close to the floor.

Most steam showers include a bench. If yours does, the steam head should be well away from the bench to minimize the risk of burns.

The other hardware item that goes in the shower is the control. The simplest are on/off switches, but options include timers and thermostats. Timers and on/off switches can be outside the shower to save you the trouble of opening the shower door to start the steam. Or you can put a set of controls inside and outside the shower. It's a good idea to have an on/off switch inside the shower in case you decide you've had enough steam before the timer finishes. If the steam starts to make you feel claustrophobic, turning on the regular shower for a minute will condense much of the steam. Controls for steam showers are low-voltage relays or air switches, so there's no risk of electrocution.

*Andy Engel is executive editor at* Fine Homebuilding.

or large glass enclosure can necessitate that you increase generator size by 25 percent to 75 percent. Each manufacturer has a chart that factors in the details to figure the size generator you need.

Drainage is another consideration. If the generator's pressure-relief valve vents, it should drain somewhere harmless. Also, most steam generators can have an automatic flushing option that cleans out the tank to minimize scale buildup. If yours has this feature, it must be connected to your home's waste drain.

## Water Goes In, Steam Comes Out

In all but the largest, most decadent of steam showers, one steam head, usually supplied with the generator, provides enough mist to trigger a foghorn. These heads are available in finishes just like other plumbing fixtures. Steam heads can even be equipped with small reservoirs that heat scented oils.

Steam heads should go near the bottom of the shower, about 6 in. to 8 in. above the floor. This placement gives the downward-

# Choosing a Lavatory Faucet

■ BY ANDREW WORMER

**H**ere's a shocker: The bathroom faucets in my house don't look like the ones in catalogs. Theirs are gleaming, germ-free, untarnished, and unsullied. My bathroom faucets are usually covered with smudges, toothpaste gunk, soap scum, and whatever else sloughs off my kids, and the faucets are usually left dripping.

The lavatory faucets at my parents' house, on the other hand, look a great deal more like the ones in the catalogs. And theirs never drip. The deal is, however, that their kids are grown, so their daily routine takes in a lot less grime than mine.

Clearly, there should be different faucets for different lifestyles. Mine should be made of titanium and contain a self-washing mechanism, like a self-cleaning oven, that clicks on every night at bedtime. Every morning, my faucets would be radiant. Until the kids woke up.

Unfortunately, if you're a parent who's in the market for a lavatory faucet, the self-cleaning type exists only in your head. There are lots of other options out there, though. You'll want to consider the type of handles—lever or traditional, depending on the strength of the hands turning the tap— the finish, the basic material it's made of, and the price.

**When choosing a faucet,** consider how it will be used. Chrome-plated solid brass is a good choice for families with young children.

## Solid Brass Forms the Best Faucet

Whatever their ultimate finish on the outside, the best faucets are solid brass on the inside. Brass is an alloy that's more or less composed of zinc and copper with small amounts of other materials such as lead. Brass is durable and corrosion-resistant, and it can be machined to close tolerances. Forged and machined brass components typically have smoother surfaces and lower lead content than cast brass, which is more porous and prone to pinhole leaks.

Less expensive faucets are made from metals such as zinc, which many refer to as "pot metal," or from thin formed steel shells that contain the necessary piping. Pot metal casts easily and has a smooth surface yet quickly corrodes in contact with water if unprotected by a plated surface such as chrome. Thin steel-shell faucets can be well made or flimsy, so put your hands on the faucet and give it a good going over before buying it.

Plastics are often used as the basic material in faucets because they are easily molded, have a smooth surface, and aren't prone to scale buildup. However, plastic-bodied faucets aren't as durable as metal and just aren't designed to last long. Also, moving parts made of plastic can wear out quickly. Plastic-body faucets cost only $10 or so; metal ones cost more.

## The Beauty of a Finish Is More Than Skin Deep

Whatever the basic material of a faucet, a critical element in its manufacture is the finish that goes on it. The most popular finish is polished chrome, which is hard and durable. Chrome, which is electrochemically deposited over nickel plating, doesn't oxidize, won't corrode, and won't easily scratch when scrubbed with abrasives.

But chrome can be deposited over plastic as well as over brass or zinc. Chrome-plated brass and chrome-plated plastic or zinc faucets look a lot alike, so much so that it can be impossible to tell what a faucet body is actually made of even when you're holding it.

Chrome plating protects the outside of inexpensive faucets for a time, but the internal workings still corrode or wear out sooner rather than later, making the more expensive brass more economical. In the same way, a chrome-plated zinc faucet won't be as durable as solid brass, but it will last

A thin plastic base plated with chrome looks like a metal faucet. List price: about $9.

Chrome plating gives this American Standard faucet a bright shine. List price: about $211.

longer than plastic-bodied faucets, which eventually lose their chrome plating.

Even most brass-finish faucets are plated. Often, chrome is applied over a solid-brass base, and then brass plating is applied over the chrome. Although these brass faucets are durable, they will oxidize in contact with air. So those beautiful, polished, brass-plated faucets need to be protected by an applied finish.

Especially for faucets in high-volume locations, steer clear of sprayed-on lacquer finishes, which are sometimes offered as a protective coating. Lacquer doesn't stand up well to bathroom cleaners or even to water.

A better choice is a clear epoxy coating, which is much more durable and resistant to scratches. But epoxy coatings are also somewhat susceptible to the solvents and abrasives sometimes used in bathroom cleansers, so in heavy-use and high-maintenance locations, a chrome finish, which won't tarnish, might be a better choice,

Another new look for bathroom faucets is colored-epoxy finishes, which are baked on, durable, and easy to keep clean. Although epoxy finishes are more durable than painted finishes, they will scratch, as I discovered when I accidentally bumped an epoxy-coated faucet against the corner of a file cabinet.

## A New Brass Finish that Won't Tarnish

Offering greater shine protection and less maintenance than traditional brass finishes is a new brass finish from both Moen® and Delta™. The finish is produced using a technology called PVD, or physical vapor deposition. Moen calls its finish LifeShine®; Delta calls its finish Brilliance®. Hans Grohe® will soon offer faucets with a PVD finish, but it's still deciding what to call the new finish. Whatever it's called, this technology is the newest thing for faucets, and other manufacturers either have a similar finish in the works or are studying the technology.

The technology for the LifeShine finish on this Moen faucet is called physical vapor deposition. List price: about $347.

Naturally, Delta and Moen have great things to say about their new finish, which will likely replace lacquered brass for all their brass faucets. They claim the finish is nearly immune to the common afflictions of brass coatings. Salt and sea air, steel wool, sprays, and powdered cleansers—even sandpaper—have no effect on the finish, they say. Do avoid getting Drano® or any product that contains lye or phosphates on the finish. And avoid Scotch-Brite® pads, warns Moen's Al Pfeninger.

One thing you should know about the new PVD brass finish is that in most cases, it's not actually brass. It just looks like brass. And as with traditional brass faucets, the new finish is actually applied over a chrome-plated faucet. Stan Nickell, Grohe's product manager, said a chrome-plated faucet is placed inside a chamber along with a colorizing substance and then subjected to high heat. The color vaporizes and "becomes part of the body," according to Nickell. "They call it 'zapping,' and it will not peel, chip, or crack. You can cut through it and won't see a trace of the chrome."

Chuck Brickell, a retired Navy admiral and nuclear engineer who's currently researching PVD at Penn State, said a variety of coating materials could produce the new brass finish. In some cases, the faucet may be brass plated and then coated with a clear

*Whatever their ultimate finish on the outside, the best faucets are solid brass on the inside.*

**Thanks to flexible hoses under the sink** that connect the valves to the spout, the handles on this Kohler IV Georges brass faucet can be set at least 8 in. apart, leaving plenty of room for cleaning around them. List price: about $800.

# One Handle or Two

In general, faucets fall into one of two broad categories: faucets that are operated with separate controls for hot and cold water, and faucets that regulate water volume and temperature with a single control.

Years ago, things weren't so complicated. Faucets were simply valves (or taps) at the end of the hot and cold water-supply lines, and any mixing of hot and cold water was done in the sink itself. But modern mixing valves with a single spout are certainly more convenient, as anyone who has tried to temper the scalding hot water from the hot side with cold water from the cold side can attest.

Faucets with individual controls for hot and cold water are known as stem faucets. Standard stem faucets consist of two valve seats (one stem for hot water, one for cold).

The standard distance between the valves of a stem faucet is 4 in., although many wide-spread faucets with widths of 8 in. or more are available. Wide-spread faucets have individual valves and separate spouts connected by flexible tubing, rather than a one-piece body like the smaller 4-in. center-set faucets. In addition, these wide-spread valves are easier for most people to use and to keep clean because there is more room between the handles. Because many sinks are often predrilled with mounting holes for the faucet, you'll have to know the faucet type when you choose your sink, or vice versa.

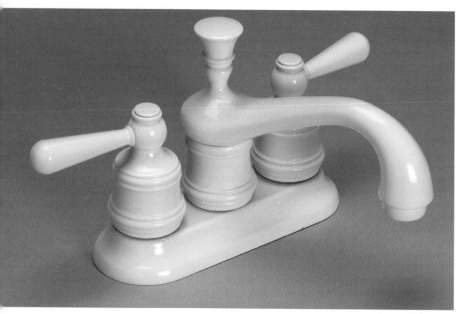

**With the valves and the spout mounted together** in a single base, this Moen faucet measures 4 in. from handle to handle. List price: about $152.

ceramic coating of aluminum oxide. Or to get a hard brass finish, manufacturers may be depositing titanium nitrite over the faucet, which produces a hard, gold-colored finish. Even better news is that the price should be the same as brass faucets.

# Lever-Controlled Faucets Take Little Effort to Control

Single-control faucets usually incorporate valves and spout in a single deck-mounted unit, and a knob or lever is used to control water volume and temperature. For the elderly, the disabled, and small children, lever-handle controls are easier to operate and require less agility and hand strength.

Ceramic-disk valving (drawings, p. 85) is the most reliable (and most expensive, initially) approach to single-control design. The control action is typically smooth and leak-free.

Lever-operated ball faucets vary a little more in performance (sidebar, p. 84). Although the better ones have balls that are machined to close tolerances, balls that are out of round will have high and low spots that make leaks more likely, and the normal grinding action of the ball against the softer valve seats will eventually wear them down, again causing leakage. Balls in this type of faucet can be either plastic, brass, or stainless steel.

Single-lever cartridge faucets that are pulled and pushed to turn on and off are relatively inexpensive and provide good performance initially. But the cartridge sleeve is continually exposed to air, water, and soap residues that wash the cartridge lubricants away and leave a residue behind. The cartridge also becomes stiffer to use, making volume control difficult, particularly for kids.

# There Are Four Main Valve Types

Regardless of the number of handles on a faucet, it's likely to have one of four basic valve types. The most basic valve is a compression valve, which has a rubber seat washer mounted on the valve stem to control the amount of water flowing to the spout (sidebar, p. 82). These valves leak when the rubber washer starts to wear out or when the valve seat becomes pitted or scratched. Replacing the washer is cheap and easy to do, and worn valve seats can be reground or replaced, if necessary.

I've found that sometimes all that it takes is a bit of polishing with 400-grit sandpaper to clean up the valve seat. This type of faucet is relatively inexpensive to manufacture and is reliable, though some consider it a nuisance to replace the washers periodically.

## Ceramic-Disk Faucets: Why Do They Ever Need Replacing?

They're the state-of-the-art in faucet valves: small, highly polished ceramic disks of various shapes that contain openings to control the flow of water. When the faucet handle is turned and the openings in the disks align, water comes out of the spout.

Ceramic disks (drawings, p. 85) are nearly as hard as diamonds and offer extreme resistance to wear. They also are highly resistant to corrosion, chemicals, lime deposits, and dirt, and they offer dimensional stability and temperature resistance. So why is it that these cartridges occasionally have to be changed?

As highly polished as ceramic disks are, their surfaces still contain thousands of tiny pores that act as reservoirs for the grease that keeps the two surfaces sealed and moving smoothly. Stan Nickell, product manager for Grohe, said ceramic-disk cartridges need occasional replacement because the silicone-grease lubricant between the two disks eventually washes away, especially on the hot-water side.

To prevent the wash-out problem, Grohe has introduced a cartridge called Carbodur. Its ceramic disks have a high-tech carbon coating and are so highly polished that silicone grease isn't needed.

Nickell assured me that ceramics themselves never wear out. They're too hard for that. But after many rotations, either the grease rinses out, the spindle wears out, or the O-ring that prevents water from spraying out around the handle wears out.

*Steve Culpepper is a former Fine Homebuilding magazine and book editor. He is currently editorial director for the shelter subsidiary of Sabot Publishing.*

# Basic Types of Faucet Valves

## 1. Compression Valves Are the Ones We Grew Up With

A threaded stem with a handle on top screws into the faucet body. On the bottom of the stem is a rubber washer that seats down into the water-supply opening. As the handle is turned, the stem is lifted from the opening, and water flows.

**Repair:** Remove the valve stem and the screw holding the rubber compression washer and replace the washer. It also may be necessary to grind the valve seat. Often, this can be done using 400-grit sandpaper.

**Cost:** For a typical washer, a few cents.

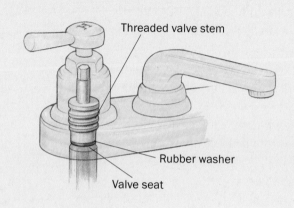

Threaded valve stem

Rubber washer

Valve seat

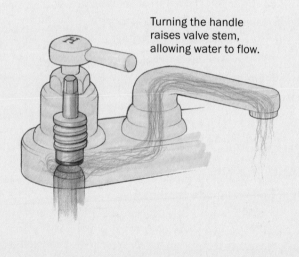

Turning the handle raises valve stem, allowing water to flow.

Some high-end manufacturers still make compression faucets. The beauty of compression faucets is their simplicity, and old faucets that are still in good functional shape—but that might need some new washers and some cleaning up—are plentiful and can be found in building-supply salvage yards, from plumbers, or anywhere you might find old fixtures, including dumps, landfills, and waste-transfer stations.

Most manufacturers in the United States have sunk a lot of money into ball, cartridge and ceramic faucets, and no longer even offer compression valves. However, European faucet makers still offer compression valves as a first choice. Europeans just don't seem to mind changing an occasional washer,

## 2. Sleeve Cartridges Take the Place of Threaded Valve Stems

These cartridges contain a hollow stem that turns inside a metal or plastic sleeve. The rubber-lined bottom of the cartridge seats into the water-supply opening. Turn the handle, and a hole in the hollow inner stem aligns with a hole in the outer sleeve so that water flows into the spout.

**Repair:** Usually the entire cartridge is replaced, but sometimes the leaking can be stopped by replacing a washer or O-ring. Occasionally, the cartridge must be pried out before it can be replaced; Moen makes a special tool for that purpose.

**Cost:** For Moen replacement cartridge in brass, about $16.75; for plastic, about $13.50.

(continued on p. 84)

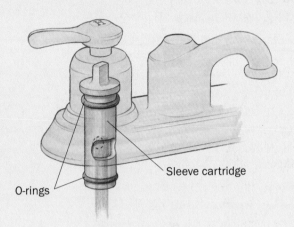

O-rings    Sleeve cartridge

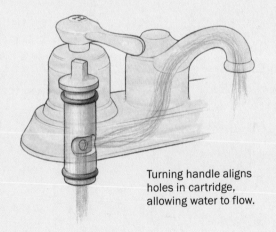

Turning handle aligns holes in cartridge, allowing water to flow.

according to Grohe's Stan Nickell (Grohe is a European company).

Peter Hemp, author of two books on plumbing, has installed just about every valve made. "My favorite would be a compression valve made by Grohe," according to Hemp.

Most manufacturers are producing stem faucets that use cartridges rather than threaded valve stems with screw-on washers. One type of cartridge is a sleeve cartridge (above). These plastic or metal cartridges (plastic cartridges are as good as brass) contain a hollow stem that's connected to the water supply. When the hole in the stem

### 3. Ball Valves Typically Have a Single-Handle Control

The valve consists of a hollow ball that contains three holes for hot and cold water supplies and one leading to the spout. When the handle is turned, one or both of the holes in the ball align with the water supply, allowing either all hot water, all cold, or a mix of the two.

**Repair:** The springs that push the rubber seats against the ball valve occasionally wear out and need replacing. Also, depending on the condition of the water, the ball itself may wear out.

**Cost:** For Delta replacement brass ball, about $7; plastic ball, about $6.50; seats and springs, about $2.35.

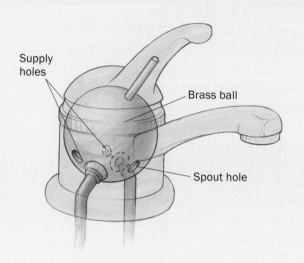

Supply holes

Brass ball

Spout hole

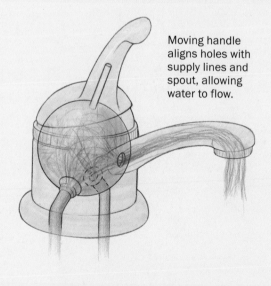

Moving handle aligns holes with supply lines and spout, allowing water to flow.

aligns with a hole in the metal cartridge sleeve, the water flows.

Another type of cartridge uses washerless ceramic disks, which are supposed to be unaffected by temperature, sediment, or minerals. The durability of the ceramic disks notwithstanding, these cartridges also contain small mesh filters that get clogged with sediment or minerals. Although ceramic valving is initially more expensive than other types of valving, ceramic disks are extremely hard and offer reliable, smooth, and consistent performance.

## 4. Ceramic-Disk Cartridges Are Simpler than They Look

The water supply and the faucet are separated by a pair of ceramic disks fixed inside a replaceable cartridge. When the handle is turned, the holes in the disks align, and water flows.

**Repair:** The ceramic disks should last indefinitely, but the O-rings, washer, and plastic parts eventually wear out, in which case the whole cartridge needs replacing. Also, the grease that lubricates the surfaces of the two ceramic disks can wash away, requiring replacement of the whole cartridge.

**Cost:** For a Kohler ceramic-disk cartridge, about $15.

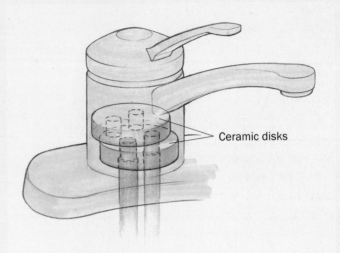

Ceramic disks

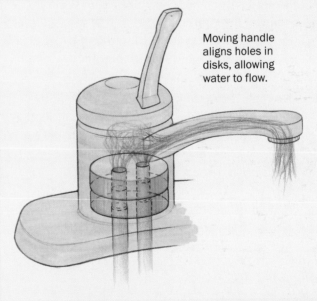

Moving handle aligns holes in disks, allowing water to flow.

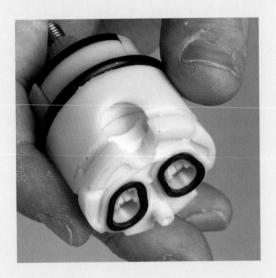

# If You're Installing the Faucet, Here Are Things to Think About

If you're not a plumber, it may be important for you to know what you're getting into before you buy a faucet. In many cases, installing a faucet means first assembling it.

For instance, Kallista's® Emperor basin set comes in more than 50 pieces, most of which have to be assembled. Obviously, with that many parts, it's important to make sure that you have all the pieces, that you keep up with all the pieces, and that you know where all the pieces go. If you're installing this faucet, the complex one-page

**Kallista's Emperor basin 8-in. spread faucet** is plated with gold and silver with a price to match. List price: $1,021 without handles; add $650 for standard handles.

*In many cases, installing a faucet means first assembling it.*

drawing of a plethora of parts that accompanies the Emperor may be hard to follow.

A much-less-expensive Moen two-handle faucet comes with a clear set of installation instructions. And it has many fewer pieces than the Kallista. Of course, anybody who shells out more than $1,000 for a gold-plated Kallista faucet probably can afford to hire a plumber.

Most one-piece faucets come nearly fully assembled. Once the trap is installed (traps are included with better faucets), the faucets are bolted to the lavatory and then hooked up to the water supply.

However, when the time comes to replace parts of your faucet—usually involving the valves inside the faucet body—where will you go to find replacements? Plumber Rex Cauldwell recommends that you stay with a name-brand faucet so that you won't have trouble finding parts when you need them.

Faucet handles are another price-related concern to keep in mind. Although most midrange and lower-price faucets come with handles, some of the more expensive faucets do not. The reasoning is that one basic faucet base can accommodate a variety of styles, so customers should be able to choose the handles they prefer. The bottom line, though, is that even after you shell out a hundred of dollars or more on a faucet, you can shell out nearly that much more for the

handles. For instance, Kallista's gold and silver Emperor faucet retails for $1,021. With handles, that price jumps to $1,671.

Another consideration that could determine the type of faucet that you buy is the kind of water you have. Minerals in hard water can build up pretty fast on metal parts. Sometimes, plastic components work better in hard water. Also, highly acidic water can eat up metal parts in a hurry, so plastic components may be what you need in that case.

Ball valves are particularly affected by sediment or by grit in water. If you're using well water, that could be a problem. Sediment also can build up or clog up any type of cartridge valve, making it more and more difficult to turn.

If you're curious about what kind of plumbing materials stand up in your area, check with a local plumber.

## Get a Faucet that Fits the Family's Use

One final point to consider before selecting a faucet: Think how it will be used. Most bathroom-faucet spouts are really too low for anything other than rinsing off a toothbrush or filling a glass of water.

For comfortably washing hands, face, or hair, a spout should really be almost 8 in. to 10 in. above the rim of the sink, and the flow of water should be directed toward the center and away from the back of the bowl, a configuration that you don't often see. Gooseneck-style faucet spouts come close to allowing these clearances, while an alternative is to include a separate deck-mounted spray head, such as you would find in a kitchen sink.

Another option is the faucet spout with an integral and detachable spray head that is also often used in kitchens. Remember that spouts that are high above the rim of the sink tend to splash if the sink basin isn't deep.

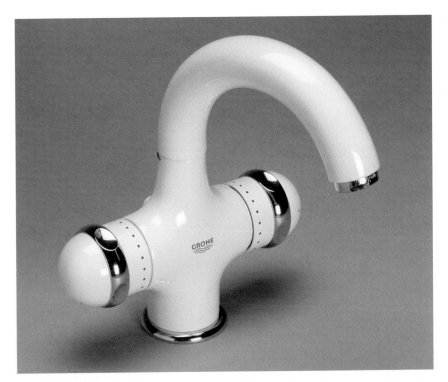

There's lots of room between Grohe's Sentossa center-set faucet and the bottom of the lavatory—room for washing your hands or face or even gulping a quick sip of water. List price: about $420.

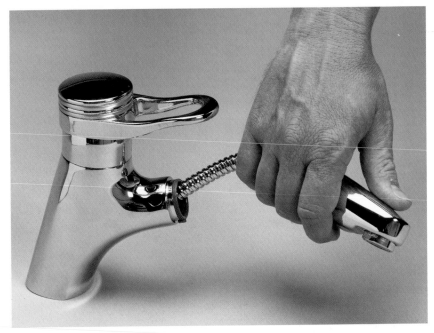

Hosing down the sink after the kids have used it and bathing the baby are just a couple of uses for Grohe's Chiara center-set faucet with a pull-out spray head. List price: about $355.

Finally, you should know that the same federal water-conservation law that mandated 1.6-gal. toilets and 2.5-gal.-per-min. (gpm) showerheads also requires that lavatory faucets release no more than 2.2 gpm at 60 psi and 2.5 gpm at 80 psi.

Different manufacturers control the flow of water from their faucets in different ways. Most faucets contain a tiny plastic screen that fits inside the aerator. Still other faucets use a regulating device located inside the valve to control the maximum flow of water.

*Price estimates noted are from 1998.

*Andrew Wormer* is a contributing editor for Fine Homebuilding magazine and the author of The Builder's Book of Bathrooms (The Taunton Press, 1998) and The Bathroom Idea Book (The Taunton Press, 1999).

# Tiling a Bathroom Floor

■ BY DENNIS HOURANY

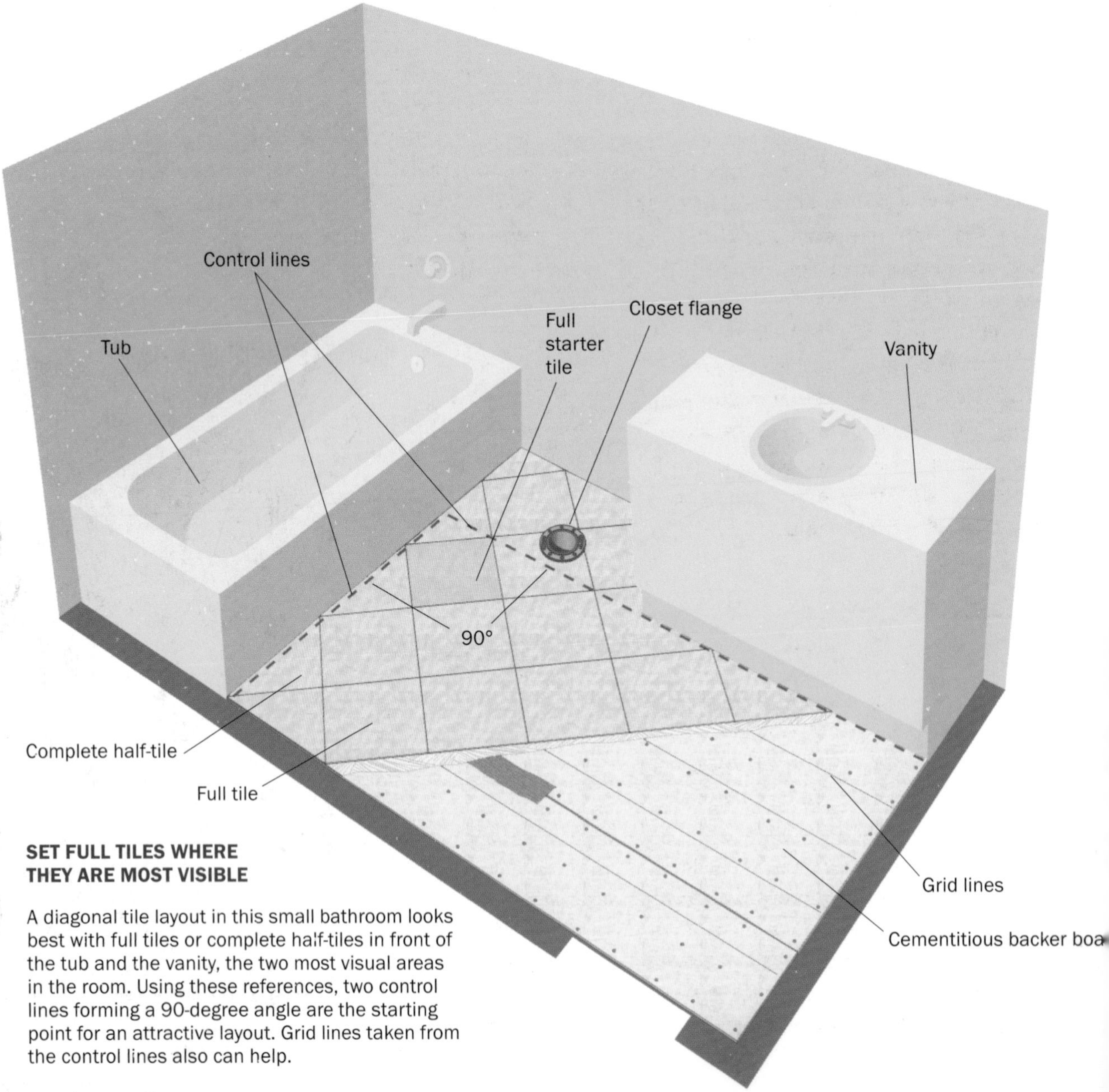

Control lines

Tub

Full starter tile

Closet flange

Vanity

90°

Complete half-tile

Full tile

Grid lines

Cementitious backer boa

## SET FULL TILES WHERE THEY ARE MOST VISIBLE

A diagonal tile layout in this small bathroom looks best with full tiles or complete half-tiles in front of the tub and the vanity, the two most visual areas in the room. Using these references, two control lines forming a 90-degree angle are the starting point for an attractive layout. Grid lines taken from the control lines also can help.

If anything can beat ceramic tile for a bathroom floor, I'd like to know what it is. Durable and nearly impervious to water damage, tile also is adaptable to just about any architectural style. The ceramic-tile industry now offers an incredible variety of tile, as well as reliable materials for setting it. If tile is more expensive than some other floor coverings, it can last as long as the house with little upkeep.

True enough, but a tile floor can be a nightmare if it is not laid out and installed carefully on a well-prepared subfloor. One of the key early considerations is the substrate on which the tile will be installed. Floating a mortar bed at least 1¼ in. thick used to be the only choice. Now we can use quick-to-install cementitious backer board.

As for the tile itself, durability and smoothness are of major concern. Most tile manufacturers rate their tiles for durability by classifying them as residential, commercial, light industrial, or industrial. For a bathroom at home, the residential grade is just fine. Smoothness is rated on a numerical scale measuring the coefficient of friction, or COF. Even though the roughness scale goes all the way to 9, I've found that a rating of 0.6 provides good slip resistance. Just keep in mind, though, that the COF goes down when the tile is wet. If you don't find the COF specified on the tile box, you can call the manufacturer for the information.

## Make Sure the Subfloor Is Flat

Setting tile on an inadequate subfloor is begging for trouble. The subfloor should meet deflection criteria set by the Tile Council of America℠—in other words, it can't have too much bounce. If it does, chances are good the tile will lose its bond with the backer board, or at least that grout joints between the tiles will crack. The Tile Council allows a maximum deflection of ¹⁄₃₆₀ of the span, or the span in inches divided by 360. For example, if you have a span of 48 in., the most sag the subfloor can show under a load is 0.13 in., or roughly ⅛ in. Although the Tile Council calls for a minimum ⅝-in. exterior-grade plywood subfloor, houses where we set tile often have subfloors of ⅝-in. oriented strand board, and we haven't had any problems. Minimum joist spacing is 16 in. o.c.

I can sense whether there is too much bounce simply by walking around on a floor. That's after setting hundreds of tile floors. When I started, though, I measured the deflection with a length of iron pipe and a dial indicator just to make sure (photo below). If there's too much deflection, don't go any farther without fixing the problem.

The subfloor also must be flat. Here, the maximum amount of leeway is ⅛ in. in 10 ft. That means if you were to lay a straightedge on the subfloor, you should not be able to see a hump or a dip that exceeds ⅛ in. A wavy floor can be corrected. One way is to use a leveling compound over the wood subfloor before the backer board is installed. You can also put the backer board down first

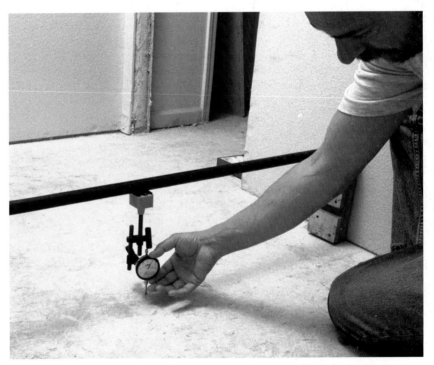

**A dial indicator attached to a length of iron pipe is one way to check whether there is too much deflection in the subfloor. A bouncy subfloor will result in cracked tile or grout.**

and then use a leveling compound that bonds to it.

In either case, the application is the same. Using a straightedge, pull some leveling compound across the low spots to fill them in. You may need to use more than one application. Leveling compounds are typically available from tile suppliers.

## When Installing Backer Board, Don't Forget to Leave an Expansion Gap

Cementitious backer board is made by several manufacturers, and it is readily available. We use ¼-in. HardiBacker® from James Hardie Interior Products. Sheets come in several sizes. I like this product a lot more than the backer board with fiberglass mesh on each side. HardiBacker cuts cleanly and easily (photo below), and it's simple to fasten to the subfloor. The ¼-in. thickness makes it easy to keep the tile at the right height, without framing a recess into the floor or having an awkward lip where the tile meets another floor surface. However, if you need to raise the level of the floor to meet an adjoining surface, you could use ½-in. cement board.

I cut and lay out all the floor's backer board before nailing any down. When it's laid out, joints should be staggered, and edges should overlap subfloor joints. It is imperative that you leave a ⅛-in. expansion gap between sheets and a ¼-in. gap at perimeter walls or other restraining surfaces, such as cabinets.

Most manufacturers require that the backer board be bonded to the subfloor with an adhesive, and we use type-I mastic. You can use thinset adhesive. But the mastic works just as well in this application, and it's faster and easier to apply (check with the backer board manufacturer before deciding what to use). Whatever the adhesive, put it down evenly with the notched trowel recommended by the manufacturer, and don't apply any more adhesive than can be covered with backer board before it skins over (top photo, facing page). I use 1¼-in. galvanized roofing nails driven into the backer board every 6 in. (bottom photo, facing page). Nail heads should be flush with the backer board, and if the floor is anything but tiny, you'll find a pneumatic nailer is a big help. We don't use screws because HardiBacker does not require them and because they are much slower to install.

**The author uses HardiBacker, a ¼-in. cementitious backer board, as a tile substrate. Scored on one side with a carbide tool, the board will snap cleanly with no back-cut.**

The author uses a type-I mastic to bond the backer board to the oriented strand board subfloor. An acrylic-modified thinset mortar also could be used.

Galvanized roofing nails 1¼ in. long should be driven 6 in. o.c. to install the backer board. Set nail heads flush with the surface.

# Set Control Lines for Laying the Tile, and Cut the Odd Ducks First

When beginning a layout, I start by checking that walls are square and parallel. If you find things are seriously out of whack and will cause many small tiles or unsightly cuts, you may consider installing the tile on a diagonal. That's what I did here, although the reason was to add a little interest to the floor, not because the room was out of square. Diagonal layouts also have the effect of making a narrow room appear wider.

Most rooms have obvious focal points where full tiles should go. I establish two control lines, 90 degrees to each other, and orient them so that they correspond with the room's focal points. For example, in the small bathroom I'm tiling here, the two crit-

Before applying thinset to the backer board, the author lays out the floor and cuts tiles to go around obstructions, such as this closet flange.

A tile saw is the most versatile tool for cutting tile. Curved cuts start with a series of straight cuts to the layout line.

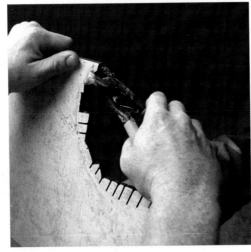

After the author makes a rough curved cut with a wet saw, he removes the waste with tile nippers.

I think it's a good idea to cut some tile in advance while the floor is still free of adhesive. I don't cut all of them, just those around the closet flange or other oddly shaped spaces. Once you get to a point where full field tiles (or cut tiles of a uniform size) will be used, cutting and fitting them in advance isn't necessary. To cut tile, I use a tile saw and a pair of nippers (photos, far left and bottom). You could use a tile board, which works by scoring and snapping tile much as you would cut a piece of glass (these tools also are called snap cutters). One disadvantage of a tile board, though, is that it can't cut L and U shapes. You can use a grinder with a diamond blade or a jigsaw with a Carborundum™ blade to cut tile. However, it's more difficult, and the cuts are not as clean.

You can't go any further without mixing up a batch of thinset mortar, which is used to bridge the seams in the backer board and to glue down the tile. I use acrylic-modified thinset no matter what the substrate. It provides a better bond, offers more flexibility, and stays usable in the bucket longer. Some kinds of tile require different thinset additives, so be sure to consult your supplier to make sure that you have the right kind.

## Preparing Thinset Requires Precision

When mixing thinset, follow the directions on the bag to the letter. One requirement is that the mixture slake, or rest, in the bucket for 15 minutes after the initial mix. Then mix it again before use. Occasional stirring may help to keep the thinset workable, but don't add any more acrylic admix or water much after the second mixing. We use a ½-in. drill to turn a mixing paddle at between 300 rpm and 400 rpm.

Taping the joints between pieces of backer board helps to prevent cracks later. We use fiberglass mesh tape 2 in. wide, bed-

ical points are in front of the vanity and in front of the bathtub; I plan on using full tiles (or complete half-tiles) in these areas. Cut tiles will go where they are less obvious. In general, I try to avoid cutting tiles to less than half their original size—they just look unsightly.

After you've determined the basic layout and the control lines, you can snap grid lines that will guide you as you set the tile. Plastic spacers will keep your grout lines a consistent width. But don't count on them entirely to keep the layout straight because tiles vary somewhat in size. Follow the layout lines, no matter what, for straight grout lines.

ding it in a layer of thinset (top left photo, p. 94). Make sure that seams between sheets are completely filled. After you apply the first layer of adhesive and tape, you'll need to put down another layer of thinset over the tape with the flat side of a margin trowel, holding it at a 45-degree angle and pressing the tape firmly into the thinset. If you tile the floor in the same day, you can tape as you go so that you won't walk or kneel in wet adhesive. But if you wait overnight, make sure not to leave any lumps of thinset at the seams.

When applying the thinset to the backer board for the tile, use the notched side and hold the trowel at 45 degress to the floor so that an even amount of adhesive is applied and no air is trapped (bottom left photo, p. 94). What you want is 100 percent coverage of both the backer board and the back of the tile, with about $\frac{3}{32}$ in. of thinset between the two surfaces. Large tiles may have uneven backs, which will require you to back-butter the surface with the flat side of a trowel. Place the tile on the thinset with a slight twisting movement to help embed the tile fully. It's also a good idea to pull a tile off the floor near the start of the job to make sure you're using enough thinset. If the back of the tile is not fully covered, you'll know to adjust your technique or trowel or both (center right photo, p. 94), assuming the thinset has been mixed properly. Look on the label of the bag the thinset comes in for the proper notch size.

If, after a while, the thinset becomes too stiff or if tile doesn't readily stick to it, throw it away and mix a fresh batch. Before the thinset dries completely, you should clean the excess from the joints (bottom right photo, p. 94). If you don't, the grout may be too thin, or it will hydrate unevenly, two conditions that make a weak grout line.

**TIP**

*Pull a tile off the floor near the start of the job to ensure you're using enough thinset. If the back of the tile is not fully covered, adjust your technique or trowel or both.*

**A mixing paddle turning at between 300 rpm and 400 rpm** does a good job of stirring up a batch of thinset. It needs to be allowed to slake, or rest, for 15 minutes before it can be used to lay tile.

Fiberglass-mesh tape bedded in a thin layer of thinset spans the gap between adjoining sheets of backer board. Skipping the tape can cause cracks to develop later.

When you're setting tile, plastic spacers will keep grout joints uniform in width, but following control lines is a better guarantee that grout lines will be straight.

The author uses a notched trowel to spread acrylic-modified thinset for the tile, taking care not to obscure layout lines.

After setting a few tiles, lift one up to make sure they have enough thinset. Large tiles such as this one may need to be back-buttered to get full coverage.

A margin trowel is a perfect tool for removing thinset that has oozed into the grout joint. If grout doesn't get all the way into the joint, the resulting bond will be weak.

## Does a Tile Look Off? Take It Out and Reset It

A day after setting the tile in this bathroom floor, I returned to apply the grout—and staring me right in the face was the corner of one tile that had sunk below its neighbors. Although the toilet would have camouflaged the problem, it was better to fix it before going any further.

Pulling a tile is not a big deal, providing you get to it before the thinset adhesive has had a chance to cure fully. In this case, the acrylic-modified thinset had been applied the previous afternoon, and it was still green. Using a hammer and a steel bar, I was able to jar the tile loose without too much trouble and without breaking the tile. After scraping the semicured thinset off the back of the tile and the floor, I applied fresh thinset to both surfaces and rebedded the tile. This time, I was careful to keep the tile flush with those around it. This repair didn't take more than a few minutes, and as soon as the tile was reset, I grouted the entire floor. You never would have known anything was amiss.

# For a High-Strength Job, Don't Overwater the Grout

Grouting can make or break the tile job. A common mistake is adding too much water or admix when mixing the grout, which causes discoloration and a weaker mix. Another is using too much water when cleaning excess grout off the tile, which also can cause it to discolor. A third common error is using a high-speed mixer for the grout, which traps air in it and makes it weak.

Add only enough water to the grout powder to make it workable. Follow the manufacturer's recommended ratio of water to grout. Ideally, the grout should be a little difficult to spread into the joints. If you're not going to mix the grout by hand, use a mixing paddle, the same type you would use for mixing thinset, and a slow-speed drill. After mixing, allow the grout to slake for 15 minutes and then remix it. At this point, you may add liquid or powder to adjust the consistency. As you work, remixing the grout occasionally will help to keep it workable, but do not add more liquid.

Use a rubber grout trowel to spread the grout diagonally, holding the trowel at a 45-degree angle (top left photo, p. 96). Grout King makes the best grout trowel I know (cost: about $13). It's worth buying one even if you use it only once.

## Sources

**Diamond Tough Tools**
614 Mountainview Ave.
Belmont, CA 94002
(888) 595-5995
www.diamondtt.com
*Grout King tools*

**James Hardie Interior Products**
26300 La Alameda,
Suite 250
Mission Viejo, CA 92691
(800) 942-7343

**Tile Council of America**
100 Clemson Research Blvd.
Anderson, SC 29625
(864) 646-1787
www.tileusa.com

Holding a grout trowel at a 45-degree angle, the author works a stiff grout mix into joints between tiles. Excess grout should be troweled off as you go.

After a single light pass across the floor, this sponge has picked up plenty of excess grout. The author flips the sponge over, makes another light pass and then rinses out the sponge.

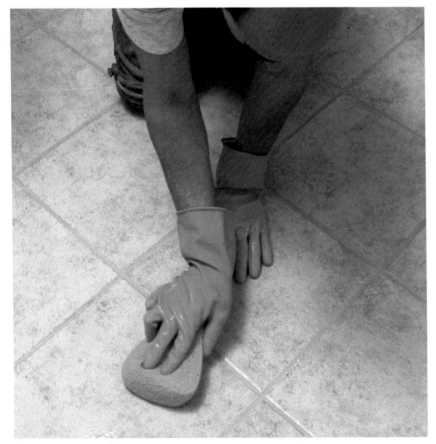

Not long after grout has been applied, a hazy film appears on the tile. That's a signal to start wiping the floor with a clean, damp sponge. Keep the pressure light.

With all the joints filled and excess grout removed with the trowel, let the grout sit until it begins to firm and you see a dry film on the tile. Then it's time to begin cleaning the tile. You'll need at least two good hydro sponges (sold at tile-supply stores) and a large bucket of clean, cool water. After wetting and wringing out the sponge, wipe the surface to get even grout joints. Then, with a rinsed sponge, use one side of the sponge for one wipe in a diagonal direction (photo left). After using both sides of the sponge, wring it out. Change the water frequently to avoid spreading dirty water on the tile. You may have to make several passes until all the residue is gone.

After the floor dries, you will see a film on the tile surface. This film can be polished off, but wait a bit until the grout is firmly set.

*Dennis Hourany* owns Elite Tile in Walnut Creek, California.

# Tiling a Tub Surround

■ BY MICHAEL BYRNE

When it comes to low cost and ease of installation, it's hard to beat the fiberglass tub-and-shower unit. It's simply slid into its berth and nailed through the flanges to the framing. When the job is done, everyone gets to bathe and shower in a synthetic shell.

I prefer standard tubs enclosed by tiled walls. Tile is not only peerless in beauty and durability, but it also can be installed with minimal expertise. Whereas tub surrounds once were tiled over skillfully prepared beds of mortar, most tile pros now favor the thin-bed method. It substitutes various prefabricated backer boards for the mortar bed, saving time and trouble without compromising durability. In this article I'll explain how to tile a basic tub surround using the thin-bed method. The job shown is a remodel, but the principles apply to new work. To satisfy the design of the room, I did two different edge treatments, one of which mimics the look of a traditional mortar-bed surround.

**Fine tuning.** After packing a wall with grout, use a damp sponge to shave high spots and fill voids.

# Framing and Waterproofing

Bathtub bays must be framed plumb, level, and square using straight stock. I add extra studs and blocking to support the edges of backer board, plus double studs to support tub enclosures, such as shower doors.

Tub surrounds need a waterproof membrane somewhere between the tile and the framing to prevent moisture infiltration. For this job, I installed economical 15-lb. asphalt felt beneath the backer board.

Before you install felt paper, it's a good idea to mark stud locations with a crayon along the top of the tub so you'll know where to fasten the backer board.

I staple felt to the studs or, if the framing is drywalled, I laminate the felt to the drywall with cold-patch asphalt roofing cement. Adjacent bands of felt are lapped shingle-style to shed water. For insurance, I also seal the joints with asphalt caulk and run a bead of caulk along the top edge of the tub to seal it to the paper.

If I'm working solo, I usually cut the top band of felt paper into two pieces for easier handling. If you do this, lap and seal the vertical joint to keep out water.

# Preparing the Backer Board

I've used mesh-reinforced cement board for more than 10 years with excellent results. It has an aggregated portland-cement core with a fiberglass mesh embedded in both sides. Panels range from ¼-in. to ½-in. thick, and they come in various widths and lengths for minimal cutting and easy handling. I sometimes use ¼-in. thick board over drywall, but I don't use board thinner than 7/16 in. over bare studs because it's too flimsy.

I cut mesh-reinforced board with a carbide scriber and grind or power sand the edges smooth. I simply mark the cutline, align the straightedge with the mark, and score the line with the scriber, making sure I cut through the mesh. Next, the board is flipped over, and the process is repeated. Then, I place a straightedge under the full length of the score, grasp the offcut, and snap it off. If the offcut is too narrow to snap, I break it off in pieces with tile biters (see the section Cutting and Drilling Tiles, p. 103).

To make small plumbing holes in mesh-reinforced board, I use a carbide-tipped hole saw. For large holes, I'll mark the opening, drill a series of ¼-in. holes around the perimeter, cut through the mesh on both sides, punch through with a hammer, and then smooth the edge of the hole with a rasp.

**Start with a solid frame.** Backer board should be affixed to a sturdy and accurately framed wall that includes studs and blocking for the backer-board seams and for the tub enclosure.

**Put a membrane under the backer board.** The author laps bands of 15-lb. roofing felt, stapled shingle-style to the studs, to keep moisture out of the wall. At vertical seams, he caulks the laps with asphalt to prevent leakage.

# Installing the Backer Board

Backer board can be hung with nails, but I prefer to use screws. They hold better than nails and put less stress on the boards during installation. I avoid regular drywall screws because their heads can snap off and because the screws can rust in a wet tub surround. I used Durock screws for this job. They come with a corrosion-resistant coating and built-in countersinks that help bury the heads flush with the panel.

I hang backer board on the back wall first, then the side walls, holding the bottom course about ¼ in. off the tub to prevent water from wicking into the board and to allow room for caulk. To speed installation, I start each screw by tapping it with a hammer before I drive it home with a power screwdriver. I space the screws according to the board manufacturer's fastening schedule and provide the recommended expansion gaps around panels.

For a contemporary look, end-wall backer board can be installed flush with adjacent drywall to allow the use of low-profile, surface-bullnose trim tiles (flat tiles with one edge rounded over). But I prefer to install the board so that it stands ½-in. proud, allowing the use of radius-bullnose trim to create the classic, curved look usually associated with mortar-bed work. To produce the ½-in. step, you either fur out the backer board or run drywall under it.

Backer-board joints get finished with 2-in. or 4-in. wide adhesive-backed fiberglass-mesh tape. In corners, I apply three overlapping strips of tape (photo bottom left). Then, I trowel the same thinset mortar over the tape that will be used for setting tiles (photo bottom right). I like to finish the joints just before I set tiles to avoid mixing an extra batch of mortar and to avoid tiling over a thinset ridge that should have been flattened but is now a chunk of stone.

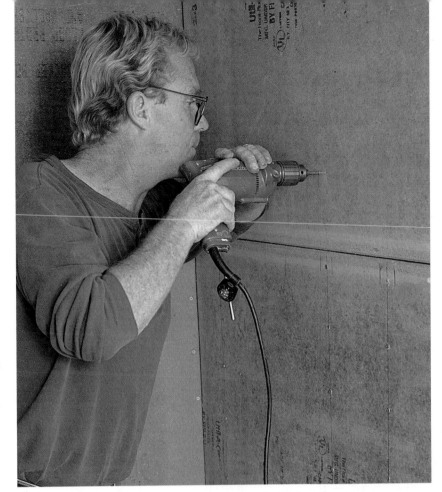

Anchor the backer board. You can use nails to affix backer board to the studs, but the board can be damaged during installation. Corrosion-proof screws are a better choice.

Tape the joints. Press self-adhering, fiberglass-mesh tape over the joints, applying three overlapping strips at inside corners.

Fill tape with thinset mortar. Use a trowel to spread thinset mortar over taped joints, forcing the mortar into the fabric of the mesh.

## Tile Layout

The ideal layout for tiled tub surrounds produces a symmetrical appearance with minimal cutting. I start by aligning several tiles along a straightedge on the floor with a ⅛-in. spacer in each joint. Although many tiles have integral spacing lugs, they typically create a grout joint that's only ¹⁄₁₆-in. wide, which I think is weak looking. I like ⅛-in.-wide grout joints because they're stronger and because they look crisp and clean. Tile spacers—X-shaped pieces of plastic—are available in various widths from any tile store. The number of tiles represents the longest run I'll have to tile—typically the distance from the top of the tub to the ceiling. I stretch a tape measure from one end of the tiles and record the distance to each joint. Correlating these numbers with actual wall dimensions allows me to plan my cuts before tiling.

**Measure the tiles.** To plan tile cuts, space a row of tiles along a straightedge, measure the distance from the end of the row to each joint and correlate the measurements with actual wall dimensions.

Back walls usually look best with identical vertical rows of cut tiles at each end. I mark the vertical centerline of the wall, plumb a level to it, and scribe a pencil line on the backer board from tub to ceiling. When laying the tile, I'll work out from the centerline in both directions. End walls need one vertical line to mark the outboard edge of the field tiles. On this job, the plumbing wall would require one vertical row of cut tiles, which could be placed in the front or in the rear. Because the opposite wall would have full tiles all the way across, I chose to put full tiles in the back to match and to cut trim tiles at the front.

Instead of drawing horizontal layout lines on the wall, I level a straightedge above the rim of the tub with shims (unless the tub is level enough to work off of, which is rare). I tile from the straightedge to the ceiling, remove the straightedge, and then fill in the bottom courses. Horizontal rows of cut tiles can be placed against the tub, the ceiling, or both, depending on personal preference (I put them against the ceiling on this job). They also can take the form of a decorative band somewhere in between.

## Mixing and Spreading Mortar

Tiles can be bedded in mastic, but you'll get better results using thinset mortar. It's a mortar-based adhesive that's mixed with water, epoxy resin, or a liquid latex or acrylic additive that increases bond strength, compressive strength, and flexibility. I use thinset mortar mixed with 4237 liquid latex mortar additive (both made by Laticrete® International Inc.). If you're worried about fussing with too many ingredients, use a powdered thinset that includes a dry polymer additive and is mixed with water. Regardless of the mortar you use, don't mix it without donning a dust mask, safety glasses, and rubber gloves. For best results, the temperature at the job site should be between 65°F and 75°F.

Although professional installers use power mixers, the strongest mortars are mixed by hand. Hand mixing doesn't infuse air into the mortar as some power mixers do. I begin by pouring all of the liquid and about 75 percent of the recommended amount of thinset powder into a clean bucket. Using a margin trowel, I mix until most of the lumps are gone. Then, I add half of the remaining powder, mix, add the other half, and mix again. You have to let the material slake (rest) for 5 to 10 minutes, then mix the batch once more until it's lump-free and ready to apply. The batch now should be plastic but not runny. I'm careful not to expose the mortar to direct sunlight (which can cook it) or to excessive air conditioning (which can dry it out). At this point the mortar should be wet enough to adhere to any surface instantly but not slip easily off the trowel.

Before applying mortar to the backer board, I wipe the board with a damp sponge to remove dust. I apply mortar with a standard notched trowel using the smooth edge to spread the mortar on the substrate and the notched edges to comb the mortar into uniform ridges. The notch size depends on the size of the tile, the condition of the substrate, and the type of adhesive you are using. The general recommendation is to use a notch two-thirds the depth of the tile. The best way to select the proper trowel, however, is to test it with the first tile you set.

## Setting Field Tiles

Bathtubs that are used constantly should be tiled with vitreous tiles, which are virtually waterproof. This tub is a backup, so I used standard 4¼-in. wall tiles having a soft, thin glaze and a porous, chalky bisque (the clay beneath the surface). They are less expensive than vitreous tiles, and they are easier to cut.

I tile the back wall one quadrant at a time, followed by the bottom half and top half of each end wall. Beginning at the back

**Wrong trowel.** Determine the right trowel-notch size by spreading mortar on a small patch of wall. Then, comb the mortar with the trowel and firmly press the tile into the mortar. Pull the tile away and assess the coverage. There shouldn't be any bare spots. This test was done with a ¼-in. by ¼-in. trowel.

**Right trowel.** Minimal squeeze-out and complete coverage on the back of this tile denote a properly sized and notched trowel for applying mortar. If mortar had oozed from the edges of this test tile, the author would have switched to smaller notches. This test was done with a ¼-in. by ⅜-in. trowel.

wall, I shim a straightedge to provide a level work surface above the tub. Then, I trowel mortar over an entire section above it (top photo, p. 102). I apply the mortar in a thick, relatively uniform layer, and I press hard to key it into the pores of the backer board. That done, I comb the mortar with the notched trowel, maintaining constant contact with the board and keeping the angle of

*Bathtubs that are used constantly should be tiled with vitreous tiles, which are virtually waterproof.*

**Spreading mortar.** Use the straight edge of the notched trowel to spread thinset mortar. Use the notched edge to comb uniform ridges.

**Setting the tiles.** With the bottom of the tile resting on spacer blocks, the author tilts each tile onto the mortar and then presses it home.

the trowel consistent to produce ridges that are uniform.

I set the first row of tiles along the straightedge. I position the bottom edge of each tile first, then tilt it forward into the mortar (a process I call "hinging"). Then, I slip a spacer between each tile, adjusting the spacing of the tiles as needed. On subsequent courses, I hinge the tiles off the spacers (bottom photo above). I lay all full tiles in a section first, then fill in any cut tiles. If the mortar skins over before a section is finished, you should recomb it. If you break the initial set by moving a tile, scrape the mortar off the tile and the substrate and apply fresh mortar. I keep a wet sponge handy for wiping goo off the surface of tiles before it hardens.

After I've tiled all the sections on a wall and all the adhesive has set up, I remove the straightedge and install the bottom courses of tile, taping them temporarily to the tiles above to prevent sagging. Because I apply mortar carefully, I don't have to seat the tiles with the traditional beating block (a padded block of wood or plywood that's laid over tiles and rapped with a rubber mallet). Instead, I use one to coax tiles gently into a smooth plane.

To enliven this surround, I installed a liner at about eye level. A liner is a decorative horizontal stripe of tile, usually less than 1-in. wide, that's used to interrupt a field of tiles. Stock liners are available in unlimited sizes and colors, but I cut my own out of matching or slightly contrasting field and trim tiles. In some cases, liners can eliminate the need to install horizontal rows of cut tiles against the ceiling or tub.

## Setting Trim Tiles

Surface-bullnose trim tiles are cut and installed just as field tiles, then temporarily taped to neighboring tiles to prevent sagging (top photo, facing page). To install radius-bullnose trim tiles, I apply a skin coat of thinset mortar to the backer board and to the flat part of the tile backs. Then, I butter the curves on the tile backs with the same grout I use for tile joints (center photo, facing page). A small amount of grout should squeeze out the ends of each tile as I push it home (bottom left photo, facing page). I lay the whole row, then nudge it into alignment with a straightedge, gently tapping the tiles flat with the trowel handle and applying tape to prevent sagging. When the grout begins to solidify, I pare the edge square to the drywall with the margin trowel.

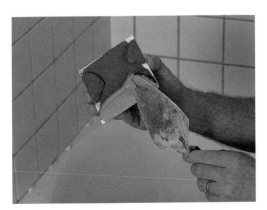

**Prevent sagging trim.** Keep the trim tiles from drooping as they set up by taping them temporarily to the field tiles. These are surface-bullnose tiles, which are used to end a row of tile when the backer board and the adjacent wall are in the same plane.

# Cutting and Drilling Tiles

The snap cutter, which you can rent from many tile stores and tool-rental shops, is the tool to use for cutting tiles down to ½-in. wide. I mark cutlines on the tiles with a fine-point, felt-tip pen, then score and break the tiles with the cutter. I then ease the resulting sharp edges with a tile-rubbing stone.

Biters are used primarily for trimming tiles to fit around plumbing (photo bottom right). They have a curved cutting edge on one side and a straight one on the other that bites into the glazed side of the tile. To make holes in the middle of tiles, I use a carbide-tipped hole saw.

For removing less than ½ in. from tiles, you have to score the tiles with the snap cutter, then nibble to the line with a pair of biters, working in from the corners of the tiles to prevent breakage. And, again, you would smooth the raw edges with a rubbing stone. To make a tile less than ½-in. wide requires a wet saw.

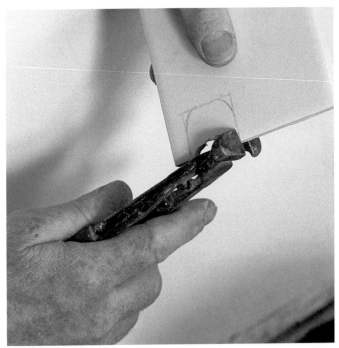

**Butter the backs.** For radius-bullnose trim, spread mortar on the flat part of the tile and grout on the curved part.

**Look for squeeze-out.** Press radius-bullnose tiles firmly enough so that grout oozes out. Remove the excess before it hardens.

**Nibble the notches.** Use a biter to notch tiles around plumbing, working in from the corners of the notch to prevent unwanted breakage.

*Only the rubber face of a grout trowel can pack joints full without scratching tiles.*

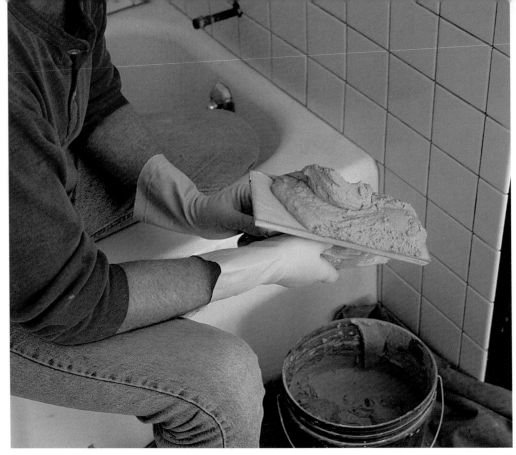

**Ready for grout. Load freshly mixed grout onto the rubber face of a grout trowel.**

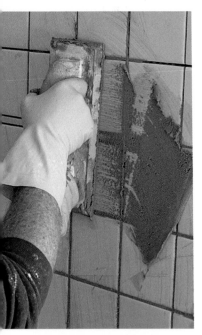

**Pack the grout. Hold the trowel at a slight angle and spread grout over a small section of wall. Work grout into joints until they are full.**

**Remove the excess. Hold the trowel nearly perpendicular to the wall and scrape off the excess grout with the edge of the trowel.**

# Grouting

Tile spacers come in various thicknesses, and some are thin enough that you can grout right over them. I prefer the thicker spacers, and I pull them out (using a dental pick) after the thinset cures. Once I've removed all the tile spacers and globs of thinset mortar from the joints, I'm ready to grout. I check the thinset container to see if there's a waiting period. If so, I wait, or the thinset mortar might stain the grout.

I use a powdered polymer-modified grout called Polyblend® from Custom Building Products® which is mixed with water. It comes in 47 colors, and the company sells caulks to match.

Only the rubber face of a grout trowel can pack joints full without scratching tiles (photo above). I start with the back wall and use the trowel to spread grout over a small section. I tilt the trowel to a 40-degree angle or less and work the grout into the joints (photo bottom left). I attack joints from three directions, with each pass cramming more grout into the joint until it's com-

**Wet cleanup.** Complete wet cleaning by making parallel strokes with a damp sponge, using a clean side of the sponge per wipe.

**Dry cleanup.** Fifteen minutes after sponging, wipe off grout haze with a dry cloth, leaving a tub surround ready for sealing and caulking.

## Sources

**Color Caulk Inc.**
723 W. Mill St.
San Bernardino, CA
92410
(800) 552-6225
www.colorcaulk.com

**Custom Building Products**
6511 Salt Lake Ave.
Bell, CA 90201
(323) 582-0846
www.cbp.com

**Laticrete International Inc.**
91 Amity Rd.
Bethany, CT 06524
(800) 243-4788
www.laticrete.com

**Miracle Sealants & Abrasives Co.**
12318 Lower Azusa Rd.
Arcadia, CA 91006
(800) 350-1901
www.miracle-sealants.com

**U. S. Gypsum**
125 S. Franklin St.
Chicago, IL 60606
(800) 874-4968
www.usg.com

pletely filled. Once all the joints in a section are filled, I hold the trowel at a right angle to the surface and rake it diagonally along the tiles to scrape off excess grout (photo bottom right, facing page). I grout the entire wall this way, packing everything except for the expansion joint above the tub and gaps around plumbing fixtures. Because grout will stiffen in the bucket, it should be stirred occasionally.

Next, I thoroughly wring out a wet, rounded sponge and gently wipe the freshly packed wall in a circular motion to shave off high spots. I avoid feathering the grout over the edges of the tiles. Then, I complete the wet cleaning by making 3-ft.-long parallel swipes with the damp sponge, using a clean face for each swipe (photo above left). At this point, I rinse the sponge after every two swipes.

About 15 minutes later, grout haze should be visible on the surface of the tile. I remove it by rubbing the tiles with a soft cloth or cheesecloth. If that doesn't work, I'll try a damp sponge or white Scotch-Brite pad.

At this stage, with the grout set up, I use a utility knife to remove the grout from the corner joint and from the ¼-in. joint I left between the tile and the tub. These expansion joints need to be filled with sealant.

After all grouting and cleaning is completed, I let the job rest while the grout cures and dries (usually about 72 hours). Then, I return to seal the grout and the raw edges of the tile with an impregnator. I use 511 Impregnator® made by the Miracle Sealants & Abrasives Company®. You have to allow the impregnator to dry before you caulk the expansion joints around the tub. I use a sealant that can be color-matched to the tile, the grout, or the plumbing fixture. It is available either sanded or unsanded (Pro-Line Class A Sealant from Color Caulk Inc.).

*Michael Byrne is the author of* Setting Tile, *published by the Taunton Press.*

# Tiling a Shower with Marble

■ BY TOM MEEHAN

**B**ack a few hundred million years or so, Earth was working overtime. Incredible forces and pressures within the planet moved continents and created mountains. Limestone, formed from the skeletons and shells of countless sea creatures, underwent an intense and miraculous transformation during this period. The result of this meta-morphosis is marble, which has become a prized building material.

While marble was being formed, various minerals and contaminants were intro-duced, producing the veins and rich colors that make each batch of marble unique. However, all of these wonderful colors make installing marble an interesting challenge.

**A hammer works like a hole saw.** The quickest, easiest way to make a hole in backer board is to pulverize the unwanted cement by tapping it with a hammer. A utility knife can be used to cut the mesh away from both sides of the board.

In 25 years as a tile installer, I have learned the importance of opening every box of marble and shuffling the tiles to get the veins and colors to work together before a project begins. My goal is to blend the tiles in such a way that the finished shower wall resembles a solid slab of marble.

The project in this article is a 7-ft. by 3½-ft. shower stall with a built-in seat and a shampoo shelf. The shower-door enclosure runs the full 7 ft. along the front of the shower bay with 1-ft. returns on both ends. This arrangement shows off the entire expanse of marble. For this particular shower, my clients chose green marble, which needs special treatment because of its chemical makeup. Green-marble tile reacts negatively to water-based or acrylic thinset cement, causing the tile to warp and break down. I avoid these problems by sealing the back of each tile with epoxy before it is installed, which I will describe in detail later on.

## Keep Backer Board off the Floor

Marble tiles for any shower should be mounted on cement backer board. For this project I used Durock, which consists of a thin layer of cement sandwiched between two layers of fiberglass mesh.

Even though backer board is not supposed to deteriorate or fall apart, it is a porous material and must be kept off the bottom of the shower floor to prevent moisture from wicking up the wall. If the backer board gets wet, it can stain the marble tile from behind. I usually keep it around 1½ in. from the floor. I also keep the nails in my backer board above the top of the shower pan or at least 5 in. from the floor to prevent the shower pan from leaking. Installing the backer board too low and nailing through the shower pan are probably the two most frequent causes of failure with a marble-tile installation in a shower.

**A showy shower out of stone.** Before installation, marble tiles are arranged so that the veins and colorations all work together. The tiles are put on as flat as possible and tight to one another to give the impression of a solid slab of marble.

**Keeping the backer board off the floor will save headaches later.** A 2x4 block is used as a spacer to hold the backer board off the shower floor. If installed too low, backer board can soak up moisture that will stain the marble from behind.

# Installing Backer Board

Cutting and installing the backer board is a lot like hanging drywall, except that all of my straight cuts are done with a special backer-board knife with a carbide blade. These knives are available for under $10 at your local tile store or at any lumberyard that sells cement backer board. I treat backer board the same as a piece of drywall, making three or four long strikes along a straightedge and then bending the sheet back and slicing the mesh on the back with a utility knife. For cutting right angles or corners, I use my grinder with a 4-in. diamond blade. Grinder cutting creates a lot of dust, so I wear a respirator and try to cut outside whenever possible.

Small holes in backer board can be drilled with a carbide-tipped hole saw. But large holes for the mixing valve and pipes are made a little differently. First I map out where I want the board removed. Then I tap at the board with a hammer until the area inside my lines has been reduced to cement dust with just the mesh on both sides holding it in place. At this point I cut away the mesh with a utility knife and remove the pulverized cement.

Before installing the board, I check the studs with a straightedge to make sure they are all in the same plane. If need be, I build out any studs that are out of line to keep the backer board as flat as possible. The backer board gets nailed to the wall every 8 in. with 1½-in. galvanized ring-shank nails. I also put in a few galvanized screws along the seams for extra reinforcement. With the board nailed in place, I finish the seams with mesh tape and thinset mortar to seal the joints and prevent future cracking and settling.

# Seal the Marble before Installation

Most marble can be put directly on the wall with regular thinset mortar, but, as I mentioned before, green marble is apt to warp and break down. Adhesive manufacturers recommend that green marble be set directly on the wall with epoxy mortar, but this procedure requires large quantities of epoxy, which is very expensive. A different solution that I've used successfully is sealing the backs of the green-marble tiles with epoxy and installing them with less expensive thinset mixed with the proper additive.

I use Latipoxy 300, made by Laticrete International Inc. The three-part Laticrete mixture comes conveniently in a can with a pair of disposable gloves and a white scrub pad for warm-water cleanup. Working with epoxy is something akin to working with saltwater taffy—sticky, messy, and tedious. So I make an extra effort to keep this part of the operation as neat and as orderly as possible. Using a flat trowel, I skim-coat the back of each tile with a thin layer of epoxy. Then I stand the tiles upright and on edge to dry, just barely touching each other.

After giving the epoxy 24 hours to dry, I scrape all of the tiles' edges with a sharp utility knife to remove any excess. Cleaning the edges will ensure that the tiles will fit together tightly when they are installed.

Once the backs of the marble tiles have been coated with epoxy, the proper thinset

**Epoxy seals the backs of the green-marble tiles.** Green marble reacts badly to water-based adhesives, so the backs of the tiles are sealed with nonporous epoxy. A trowel spreads the thick and gooey epoxy.

must be used to bond the tiles to the walls and floor. Plain thinset or thinset with a basic acrylic additive is fine for regular marble and might seem to work initially for the epoxy-coated tiles as well. But the longevity of a bond between regular thinset and epoxy is questionable. The thinset must be mixed with an additive specifically designed for bonding to a resilient surface such as vinyl or linoleum flooring. This mixture will also bond to the nonporous epoxy coating on the marble. For this project the additive I used was MAPEI® Ultra Set 2. Another thinset/additive combination that I have used successfully in this application is Laticrete thinset cement with Laticrete 333 liquid additive.

## Start the Tiles Out Level with Ledger Board

The two main objectives when installing marble tile are keeping the joints between tiles tight and making the walls a continuous flat, even plane.

I took great pains ahead of time to build this shower stall in even 12-in. increments. This careful planning kept my cut tiles close to full size. I laid out the shower with full-width tile for the top course against the ceiling and cut tile on the bottom course along the floor. Rather than begin my tile installation with the cut course, however, I opted to start with the first course of full-width tiles. To keep this starter course perfectly level, I tacked a ledger board on the wall along the bottom edge of the course of tile (photo right). This ledger board also provided some support for the heavy marble tiles while the adhesive was curing.

I began by spreading my thinset mixture on the walls with a ⅜-in. notched trowel, covering enough of the wall for two courses. Then I buttered the back of each tile before it went on the wall. With this amount of thinset, I can push a tile in or build it out as needed to keep the wall perfectly flat. Two

tools that come in handy for this process are a rubber mallet and a large suction cup with a release switch, available at tile stores, glass shops, or marble-supply stores. I use the mallet to tap tiles in and to keep them tight to one another, and the suction cup lets me pull a tile out and reset it if it's in too far. Keep in mind that, unlike ceramic tile, marble has a square outside edge that becomes visible with the slightest bit of unevenness in the installation. After setting the first three courses on the back wall, I moved to the side walls to give the thinset a chance to set a little before adding the weight of the additional courses.

### TIP

After setting the first three courses on the back wall, move to the side walls to give the thinset a chance to set a little before adding the weight of the additional courses.

**A ledger board keeps the starter course level.** A length of 1x is leveled and tacked to the wall to provide support and alignment for the starting course of tile.

Thinner tiles are used to build out the decorative band. Full-size tiles are cut into smaller squares, then cut in half again. A complementary color was chosen for the diamond. Instead of giving these smaller tiles a thick bed of mortar, thin and unglazed tiles were used to shim them out to the plane of the rest of the wall.

## Create a Decorative Border

To minimize the cold, formal look a large marble shower stall can sometimes have, my client decided to add a decorative band just above the fifth course of tile. To create this border, I used my wet saw to cut a bunch of the sealed green tiles and several beige marble tiles into 4-in. squares. Then I cut each of the 4-in. green tiles in half diagonally and created a two-tone diamond band that runs around the perimeter of the shower. At the corners of the shower stall, I used half of a beige diamond going in both directions to give the appearance of a folded tile.

Building these small tiles out to the same plane as the rest of the wall can present a problem. I had used a fairly thick layer of adhesive to keep the 12x12 tiles flat. This method can get pretty sloppy and difficult when building out small tiles. So I used some leftover unglazed mosaic tiles as shims to bring the smaller decorative pieces out flush with the field tiles. The thinset adhesive had no problem adhering to mosaic tile because both sides of the tile were unglazed.

## Bullnose the Tiles with a Saw and a Grinder

I bullnosed, or rounded the edges of, all of the tiles for the outside corners of the shower stall to soften the edge. I own a water-fed router, but it was in the repair shop when I was working on this project. Because the router is both wet and loud, I try to use it only if I have a lot of bullnosing to do. Instead of the router, I used another method that's a bit slower and requires a little more patience but that gave the same great results.

First I run a tile through my tile saw, holding it at a 45-degree angle, removing only about ⅛ in. from the edge of the tile. After making this cut on several tiles, I set up five or six in a row on the edge of a table or bench. I use a grinder or spin sander with 80-grit paper to round off the two edges of the chamfer and create the bullnose on all five tiles at once. Then I polish the rounded edge with sanding disks, working progressively up to 600 grit.

Diamond pads soaked in water can also be used to create the bullnose after chamfering. These pads make less dust and work better on marble than regular sanding disks. Diamond pads come as a six-part, color-keyed, graduated-grit system that can be purchased from most marble-supply houses. When I've worked through the finest grit, I rub a little marble polish on the bullnose as a final step.

## Smaller Tiles Are Better for the Shower Floor

It's possible but not practical to use 12-in. tile on the shower floor. So again I cut full-size tiles into 4-in. squares. Using smaller tiles not only makes it easier to match the gradual pitch of the shower pan, but it also increases the number of grout joints for better traction on the slippery marble surface.

I spread my thinset on the floor with a ¼-in. notched trowel for the smaller floor tiles. Because of the slope of the shower floor and the ample size of the grout joints, I didn't need to butter the backs of the tiles with thinset. To add a little character to the floor, I used triangular tiles around the

**Tiling is tough on tools.** A framing square is used to check the alignment of the floor tiles and to keep them running straight. But it's hard to do without plunking the tool down in fresh adhesive, which isn't great for the square.

perimeter, which put the field tile on the diagonal. Because the shower floor was so large, I checked my rows of tile often with a framing square and a straightedge to keep everything straight and even (photo above).

## A Built-In Corner Seat and Shampoo Shelf

When I was installing the backer board for the shower seat, I extended it 1½ in. higher than the top of the framing, which was covered with the waterproof membrane. Instead of putting backer board on top of the seat, I filled the extra 1½ in. with a bed of cement so that there would be no nails directly under the horizontal surface of the seat. This technique is a great way to avoid staining and leaks down the road. I also gave the cement a good ¼-in. pitch away from the walls so that water would run off the seat easily. Instead of tiles, I used a marble slab that I got from a marble supplier for the top of the seat. The solid piece of marble not only looks better than a course of tiles, but it also provides seamless waterproofing for one of the most vulnerable areas of the

shower stall. The top of the shower threshold also received a similar treatment.

I laid out the built-in shampoo shelf after I installed the first three courses of tile so that the shelf would land directly above a full-tile course. I cut the opening for the shelf in the backer board with my grinder. The shelf cavity was framed with lengths of 2x4 that I stuck in with dabs of mastic. The mastic held the framing in place until I could screw through the board to attach the framing permanently. As I did with the seat, I pitched the bottom shelf to shed water, but not enough to let the shampoo bottles slide out.

## Clean Marble with a pH-Neutral Solution

After the marble was installed, I grouted the whole shower with a forest-green grout. It's a good idea to test the grout on a tile scrap to make sure that it won't stain the marble. I mixed my grout the way I usually do, using plain water, and I spread the grout with a float and a stiff, damp sponge. Even though

## TIP

*Test grout on a tile scrap to make sure that it won't stain the marble.*

**The marble for the seat goes on top of cement.** The backer board around the shower seat was left 1½ in. high, and then the resulting cavity was filled with cement, making the seat top virtually waterproof. A marble slab was used for the seat to eliminate grout joints.

## Sources

**Laticrete
International Inc.**
91 Amity Rd.
Bethany, CT 06524
(800) 243-4788
www.laticrete.com

**MAPEI Inc.**
White Head Ave.
P.O. Box 105
South River, NJ 08882
(800) 426-2734
www.mapei.com

**ProSoCo**
3741 Greenway Circle
Lawrence, KS 66046
(785) 865-4200
www.prosoco.com

**United States
Gypsum Co.**
125 S. Franklin St.
Chicago, IL 60606
(800) 874-4968
www.usg.com

the wall tiles are a tight fit, I go over them to fill any hairline gaps that might be left. The grout joints between the marble floor tiles are filled the same as with ceramic tile.

I give grout a couple of days to cure before I clean the tile. Marble is sensitive to acid, so it must be cleaned with a pH-neutral cleaning solution. There are several marble cleaners on the market, and they're available at most tile stores. Avoid acidic cleaners such as vinegar, which can etch the surface of the tile and strip it of its finish. I give the marble a final rinse with clean water even after using a cleaner made for marble.

Most marble in a heavily used shower will require maintenance. Lighter marble is particularly vulnerable to staining, but all marble needs to be kept properly sealed. Two weeks after the installation, I seal the marble with an impregnator/sealer called Limestone Marble Protector made by ProSoCo Inc.® This product seals the microscopic pores of the stone. It doesn't change the appearance of the marble, but it helps to repel water and to prevent deep staining. I always test the sealer on a scrap of whatever

marble I've used in a project. It's best to leave it overnight to make sure there are no adverse chemical reactions on the surface of the marble. Finally, I go over the shower walls with marble polish, which offers additional protection from soap and shampoo and gives the marble a nice, even finish.

*Tom Meehan is a second-generation tile installer and owner of The Cape Cod Tileworks, a tile store in Harwich, Massachusetts.*

# Tiling with Limestone

■ BY TOM MEEHAN

**M**y wife, Lane, and I own a tile store on Cape Cod, so I've gotten used to seeing tile of many different colors, shapes, and materials all in the same room. But I've never met a homeowner who wanted to turn a bathroom into a tile showroom. I did come close recently when I tiled a bathroom that combined striking black marble, gray granite, tumbled marble, and a large, colorful hand-painted ceramic mural. The unifying element that made this unlikely combination successful was limestone tile.

## Sort the Tiles before You Mix the Mortar

As an experienced tile installer, I had the dream job of integrating all these different types of tile with limestone in a single room. Limestone, which can be fairly soft and porous, is usually a breeze to work and has subtle, earthy tones that form a perfect complement to almost any type or color of material.

Because the color of limestone can vary from tile to tile and from box to box, I begin by opening boxes and checking the tiles for differences in shade or slight veining that might make one tile stand out from the rest.

The differences are usually subtle, but a misplaced tile in a different shade can stick out.

As I went through the boxes of limestone tiles for this bathroom, I culled some tiles that had slightly different shades or that had chipped corners. I also came across some tiles with nice crystalline veins that I set aside to give large open areas such as the floor or the shower walls a monolithic look. Out of the 550 sq. ft. of limestone tile that I installed in this bathroom, only about 20 or 30 tiles were irregular in color or badly chipped. These tiles were set aside for cuts, and tiles with off colors were relegated to an inconspicuous closet floor.

To add interest to the layout, we decided to run the tiles diagonally on the horizontal areas (tub deck and main floor). The diagonal pattern contrasted the square layout of the wainscoting and the shower walls. For the floor, I figured that a 6-in. border (in black marble) would allow me to use more full tiles and fewer small pieces in the field.

To enhance the diagonal layout, I positioned 3-in. black-marble inserts at the intersection of every fourth tile. A pattern of inserts done this way is called a clipped-corner pattern because the corners of the intersecting tiles are cut off to accommodate

**Applying a sealer.** Brush on a final coat of sealer once all the tile is grouted.

the insert. I centered the floor pattern in the area that would be seen first, in front of the raised-panel tub-enclosure face.

Another layout concern was the long exposed wall that holds the main door to the bathroom. To catch another full diagonal tile, I increased the border along that wall to about 6½ in. My objective was to give the appearance that the room was built to the size and dimension of the limestone tile.

The layout of the walls was relatively simple. Because the floor tiles ran diagonally, the walls and floor did not have to line up. I made it a point to avoid small cuts whenever possible and to put the fuller-cut tiles in obvious places such as inside corners. The mural was centered on the wall above the tub to give the feeling of looking out a big limestone and ceramic window at Cape Cod's scenic landscape.

# A Wet Saw Is Indispensable

Working with limestone is similar to working with polished marble. However, marble is much less forgiving and is usually set in a perfect plane with no grout joint. In most cases, however, limestone can look better with a fine grout joint. On this job, I left a ⅛-in. joint between the tiles.

Because limestone is part of a geological formation (sedimentary rock), it should be cut only with a wet saw equipped with a diamond-edge blade (photo right). I precut as many pieces as possible, especially when the tile is being installed in a diagonal pattern.

As with most tiles, limestone seems to bond best either to a good cement backer board or to a cement-and-sand-based mud job in wet areas such as the shower and tub. Limestone also bonds well to drywall in areas where water isn't a concern. I did a mud job on the shower floor and used backer board for the shower walls and for the tub deck running up the walls a foot or so. For the rest of the wall work, I installed

## Limestone's Origins: Fossils, Coral, and Seashells

Look at limestone under a microscope, and you'll see coral, seashells, and the skeletons of sea creatures that accumulated over eons in the sediment on the ocean floor. Millions of years ago, the surface of the earth was changing dramatically. Mountains were thrust up out of the oceans, and the sediment on the ocean floor turned into limestone. Some of that limestone encountered tremendous geological heat and pressure, crystallizing and transforming it into marble.

Like marble, limestone occurs in a wide variety of textures and colors from grays, greens, and reds to almost pure white. Far and away the most common color of limestone tile is a sandy beige like the tile used here. Even so, a single tile can have specific areas of contrasting color, and often you can see the full outline of a seashell or fossil in limestone's richly textured surface.

*A wet saw is the best tool for cutting limestone, but installation is similar to regular tile.*

**TIP**

*Regular gray thinset has a tendency to darken the light-colored limestone, so always install the tile with white latex-modified thinset.*

**Wet-saw jig from a tile scrap.** A discarded tile cut at a 45-degree angle and clamped to the wet saw's sliding table streamlines cutting tiles for a diagonal layout.

**Buttered back for better adhesion.** Because of limestone's porous nature, the back of every tile receives a thin layer of mortar, a process known as buttering, which ensures sound attachment for each tile.

**No special mortar for limestone.** After the backs are buttered, the limestone tiles are set in the same latex-modified mortar used for many other types of tile. The lighter color was chosen because darker mortars can darken the limestone permanently.

back with a thin layer of thinset (photo top left). This step may be slightly overkill, but it is cheap insurance for achieving a 100 percent bond when the tile is set in place.

## Limestone Can Be Shaped with a Grinder and Sandpaper

When I'm installing an outside corner with ceramic tile, I have to order special tiles to achieve the bullnose edge. With stone tiles such as marble and limestone, edges can be carved or ground right into the edge of regular tiles. With polished marble, that edge has to be polished with a series of abrasive disks that get progressively finer. However, with limestone, once the bullnose edge is roughed out, I just go over it with 80-grit sandpaper to fine-tune the shape and then 120-grit sandpaper to smooth the finish. If I go any finer with the sandpaper, I have to be careful not to make the edge more polished than the tile itself.

One challenge in tile work made easy with limestone is forming tiles for an arched opening like the one I did over the shower entry in this bathroom. The first step was scribing the arched opening onto plywood for a template. Then I set a compass at 4 in. and paralleled my scribe line to form the arch. After cutting out the arch template, I traced the shape onto three pieces of limestone (top left photo, facing page).

It was easy to follow the outside radius of the arch with the wet saw, but the inside radius was challenging. I sawed over to the inside-radius line and removed the bulk of the waste. I then used my grinder to cut to the line.

The top of the radius still had to be bullnosed. The best way to put an even edge on a series of tiles is to join them together in the same order as they will be installed. For a square edge such as an outside corner of a wall, I just line up the tiles against a straightedge on the worktable and mold them as a single entity.

the limestone over the mildew-resistant drywall on the walls after priming the drywall with a skim coat of thinset the day before installing the tiles.

One often-overlooked characteristic of limestone is its translucence. Regular gray thinset has a tendency to darken the light-colored limestone, so I always install the tile with white latex-modified thinset. For this job I used Laticrete International 253, a polymer-modified thinset mortar that mixes with water.

I spread the mortar for these limestone tiles with a ⅜-in. notched spreading trowel. Before installing each tile, I buttered the

**Cut tiles are glued temporarily to the template.** After the tiles are cut, the author glues them to the template. Having the tiles aligned the way they will be installed makes it easier to keep the edge shape consistent.

**A grinder roughs out the bullnose.** An abrasive pad on an electric grinder fairs the curve of the arch and rounds over the tiles. A quick pass with 80-grit and then 120-grit sandpaper gets the tile ready for installation.

**Arched door trim starts with a plywood template.** After scribing the arch of the shower entry onto a piece of plywood and adding the top edge of the tile trim, the resulting shape is transferred to the limestone.

The arch, however, was a more formidable task. I began by gluing the pieces of limestone to the plywood template (photo top right). I used a glue called Akemi® from Axson® North America Inc., a quick-setting two-part polyester used to join stone to stone. In that capacity it forms a tenacious bond, but because I was gluing to plywood, I was able to break the bond and chip off the glue when I was finished shaping. Next, I used an electric grinder to round over the top edge of the arch to form half of a bullnose (photo center). After I finished the edge with sandpaper, the tiles were installed with the preshaped edge forming a continuous curve (photo bottom right).

**The arch goes up.** Once the tiles are shaped and smoothed, they are installed on the wall, leaving the proper spacing for an attractive grout joint.

# A Mural in a Field of Stone

The crown jewel of this bathroom is a hand-painted ceramic-tile mural by Pat Wehrman of the Dodge Lane Potter Group in Sonora, California. The mural—done in three sections—depicts a salt marsh with cattails and great blue herons, the same view someone is likely to have looking out the large bay window over the tub. Even though the individual pieces in each section were large, the mural went together like one of the jigsaw puzzles my sons love to play with.

I'm always extra careful handling the pieces of a mural. If a piece gets lost or broken, it is nearly impossible to replace it with one that will match the original both in size and in color.

Each section of the mural came with a map to help us reconstruct it accurately (photo right). First, James Mahony, my assistant, dry-fit all the sections together on a large sheet of plywood while I put layout lines on the wall. Next, I set the limestone tile on the wall up to where the mural would begin. Starting at the lower right-hand corner, I worked up and across each section of the mural.

I set the mural tiles in the same white thinset I used for the limestone (photo facing page). Because of the irregular shapes and sizes of the mural pieces, I spread the thinset with the same ⅜-in. by ⅜-in. notched trowel. As each section was completed, I moved the pieces with my fingertips until the grout joints were perfect. A few strategically placed plastic wedges helped to keep the pieces from drifting back (photo right).

The final installation step was adding the limestone frame around each section. The limestone was sealed, grouted, and sealed again. Magically, as the limestone around the mural dried, the subtle colors in the stone enhanced and magnified all the hues in the hand-painted glaze of the mural.

**With the help of a paper map provided by the artist, the installer lays out the ceramic-tile mural carefully on a sheet of plywood.**

**When all the sections are set in place and framed with limestone, a final rinse and wipe down removes excess mortar from the hand-painted ceramic surface.**

**After it is laid out, the mural is assembled from its lower corner; the installer works up and over until each section is completed.**

The first coat of sealer. Sealing before the grout is spread keeps the tiles from absorbing the liquid in the grout and keeps the grout from staining the tiles.

**TIP**

*If you discover scratches or marks on the limestone that won't disappear with regular cleaning, hit those areas lightly with 120-grit or 220-grit sandpaper. After sanding reapply a coat of sealer.*

# Seal Twice, Grout Once

Cleaning and sealing the limestone before grouting is a must. At this stage, limestone should be sealed with a coat of an impregnator sealer to protect it from staining and to act as a grout release before grouting (photo above). Manufacturers suggest testing the sealer on a small area of stone first. A good impregnator should not darken stone but leave it in its natural state when it dries. I try to seal the edges of the tile as well so that the porous limestone doesn't suck the moisture out of the grout and cause it to cure prematurely.

I've used two different sealers: Miracle Sealants Porous Plus and StoneMasters™ Gold Seal®. I usually apply the sealer with a foam brush and then wipe down the tile with a clean rag. These sealers give off organic vapors, so if you're not installing the limestone in a well-ventilated area, I recommend wearing a respirator.

I grouted the limestone with a latex-modified floor grout made by TEC®. For these ⅛-in.-wide grout joints, I chose a sanded grout. Once the tile had been sealed and dried 24 hours, I grouted in pretty much the same way I do for most other tiles, raking the grout in diagonal strokes across the grout joints to ensure that they get completely filled. When I'm grouting limestone, though, I try not to spread or cover more than 40 sq. ft. to 50 sq. ft. at a time. If any places in the grout joint did not get sealer, the grout could cure too quickly, making it difficult to work and also reducing its strength.

# A Cleanup before the Final Sealer

I waited two or three days to let the grout cure completely and then cleaned the tile thoroughly with a pH-neutral cleaner. Your local tile store can steer you toward several different cleaners. I then let the tile dry for a

# Waterproofing Membrane for a Built-In Shower Niche

A lot of the showers that we tile these days call for a tiled alcove or niche for shampoo bottles and soap. Most often, we line the framed opening with backer board and install the tile right on top. However, if I know that there is the possibility of a lot of water pressure hitting the niche directly, I line the backer board with a waterproof membrane. We decided to go that route with the niches in this shower.

The system we used here is made by Laticrete. After taping and sealing the backer-board corners and seams inside the niche with thinset mortar, my assistant, James Mahony, began the membrane by applying a coat of Laticrete 9235 waterproofing liquid, a black self-curing latex-rubber compound, over the whole interior of the niche. He took care not to get any black on the finished limestone walls of the shower. The compound is pretty noxious, so James wore rubber gloves and a respirator while installing the membrane, especially in the confines of the shower stall.

Next, a nonwoven polyester fabric supplied with the kit was pressed into the wet compound (top photo). James trimmed the excess out of the corners and then applied another coat of the black compound, thoroughly saturating the fabric (center photo). The compound combines with the fabric to create the waterproof membrane. The next day, James installed the limestone in the niche using a latex-modified thinset, also made by Laticrete, as an adhesive (bottom photo). Even with the waterproof membrane, we pitched the bottom of the niche slightly so that water would run out easily.

Fabric is pressed into the wet liquid. After the inside of the shampoo niche is coated with a latex-rubber liquid, a nonwoven polyester fabric is pressed into the liquid.

A second coat of latex-rubber saturates the fabric. When the fabric has been installed, a top coat of rubber-latex liquid is applied to impregnate the fabric thoroughly.

Tiling the niche. After allowing the membrane to cure overnight, the limestone tile is then set into the same latex-modified thinset used in the rest of the room.

## Sources

**Axson North America Inc.**
www.axson.com

**Dodge Lane Potter Group**
Sonora, CA
(209) 532-3876
*Pat Wehrman, designer of mural*

**Laticrete International Inc.**
91 Amity Rd.
Bethany, CT 06524
(800) 243-4788
www.laticrete.com

**Miracle Sealants Company**
12318 Lower Azusa Rd.
Arcadia, CA 91106
(800) 350-1901
www.miracle-sealants.com

**The final coat of sealer.** When all the tile is installed and grouted, a second coat of sealer is applied over the entire tiled surface. Sealer keeps the limestone from staining.

**Protecting limestone from dark grouts.** Here, the light-colored limestone has been masked off while black grout is applied to the marble border.

week or more, depending on the humidity, before applying the final coat of sealer. Some sealer manufacturers recommend that you wait 30 days before sealing to make sure all the moisture is released from the stone. Unlike other sealers, an impregnator sealer allows the tile to breathe and to release its vapors after the sealer is applied.

The French limestone in this bathroom is highly porous, so I doubled the final coat of sealer on the floor and tripled it on the tub deck and in the shower. When sealing shower walls, I start at the bottom and work my way up to prevent the sealer from streaking. I also make sure that I don't leave pud-

dles of sealer on flat surfaces. Pooling sealer can darken and glaze over limestone.

The black grout that I used on the marble border can seriously stain the limestone. So after the limestone is sealed, I mask it off before spreading the black grout (photo above right).

Should you discover scratches or marks that won't disappear with regular cleaning, hit those areas lightly with 120-grit or 220-grit sandpaper. Once I have sanded a tile to remove a mark, I then reapply a coat of sealer.

*Tom Meehan is a second-generation tile installer and owner of The Cape Cod Tileworks, a tile store in Harwich, Massachusetts.*

# Silicone Caulking Basics

■ BY BRIAN ZAVITZ

**S**ealing a bathroom fixture, kitchen fixture, or ceramic tiles with silicone caulk is one of those small details that—done well—raises a job above an ordinary level. I don't know how many times I've seen the effect of a good tiling job—and sometimes even a superior one—spoiled by sloppy caulking.

Proper silicone caulking accomplishes two things. It prevents water from finding its way into the gaps where two surfaces meet, with enough flexibility to maintain the integrity of the seal even if the materials shift a bit over time. And when the caulk is smooth and even, it helps to prevent the accumulation of dirt and mildew outside the seal, which helps to maintain the aesthetics of the job over time. A workmanlike job accomplishes the first purpose, but it requires more practice and care to accomplish the second.

Silicone caulk is the caulking of choice for ceramic tile, showers, tubs, sinks, and other bathroom and kitchen fixtures. It costs more than latex caulk, but it lasts longer—up to 20 years. It's a rubbery material with a tenacious grip, so it does a better job of stretching and flexing. Because it stretches without cracking or splitting, it does a better job than latex of sealing out water that inevitably accumulates next to kitchen and bath fixtures. Also, it has a wide temperature-application range and can withstand temperatures from below 0°F to about 400°F.

The drawbacks include silicone caulk's finicky nature when it's being tooled and its reluctance to adhere to painted surfaces, plastics, or oily woods. Also, silicone caulking is generally not paintable.

## Start with the Right Stuff

The basic caulking tool is, of course, a caulking gun, but even here a little care is needed. A gun that operates with ratchet action is no good for fine work. With ratchet action, you have to release the trigger and reach around

to the back, grab the end of the rod and twist it to relieve pressure in the tube. In that time, it's easy for excess material to squeeze out, and the action can cause the tip to jerk, which spoils the bead.

Instead, find the type with a (usually) hexagonal rod and no notches, which is released by pressing your thumb on a tab behind the handle. This type of caulk gun delivers caulk with a smoother flow, and the pressure can be released instantly so that you won't have to take your eyes or your hands away from the work. (Tub and tile caulk in a squeeze tube works only on very small jobs. There's just not enough caulk there to give a long and consistent bead.) Some caulk guns have a spout cutter that is incorporated in the handle, but I prefer to cut the spout cleanly with a sharp knife.

All silicone is not the same, either. Some caulks are firmer than others coming out of the tube, and some skin over faster. Some are more flexible when cured or come in more colors. GE's® silicone, the granddaddy of them all, is still among the best. I find it easy to work, strong, and flexible, and I like the opaqueness of its white. I also find that the white yellows a bit, so when working with pure-white tiles, I prefer to use another brand, such as Hilti. Whatever brand you choose, always get the type specifically made for tub and tile work, which contains compounds to inhibit mildew.

Choosing a color when the job calls for something other than white can be tricky. Almond (or bone) and gray are the most common variations, but manufacturers offer widely differing renditions of those colors. If a close match is important, I often buy tubes of a few different brands, then squeeze out test beads on-site to make a final choice. Usually, an exact match is impossible, in which case I prefer a color slightly darker than the material I'm applying it to.

One expedient is using clear silicone, but that's a last resort for me for two reasons. First, if there's a fair-size gap at the joint, it remains visible after the caulking is done.

**The basic tools are pretty basic.** A decent caulking gun—the type with a hexagonal rod and thumb-tab release—a spoon, a utility knife, a scraper, a brush, and cleaners are all you need to do a first-rate caulking job. Also bring along plenty of paper towels for cleaning up.

Also, after tooling clear caulk, I may not be able to see some smears or excess, but they sure will show up once the bead gets dirty. Nevertheless, for some jobs, particularly against varnished or unfinished wood or where you have materials of different colors meeting, clear may be the best solution.

## Prepare the Area to Be Caulked

Proper preparation of the area to be caulked is especially important with silicone. Even with a brand-new installation, I make sure the surfaces are clear of dirt, excess glue, or silty deposits of grout. When remodeling, the big enemies are soap, scale, and mildew.

If I'm recaulking, I start by cutting out all the existing silicone with a utility knife, then scraping the surface clean with one of those paint scrapers that holds a single-edge razor. Next I scrub the whole area with a bit of wood alcohol. It does a good job of dissolving soap deposits, and it's also the least toxic thing I know of that will dissolve uncured silicone (nothing I know of dissolves cured silicone). This comes in handy later if I need to clean up stray silicone. If the area to be caulked is really scaly or particularly disgusting, I'll scrub it with a weak solution of muriatic acid or trisodium phosphate (TSP).

If there is still some mildew remaining in the grout, I may wash it with bleach or even rake out the grout and redo it. After making sure that the whole area is clean and dry and that any traces of the wood alcohol have evaporated, I'm ready to start. Before cutting the tip of the caulking tube, though, I always have a plentiful supply of paper towels close at hand. Silicone caulking can be pretty messy.

## Start with the Smallest-Possible Bead

I cut the tip of the tube spout on an angle, as close to the end as practicable for the job. It's all too easy to get too much caulk on the work, and all too hard to get rid of it neatly if you do. So I work with the absolute smallest bead that will fill the gap. Silicone-caulking manufacturers say there is no minimum-size bead, although they don't recommend beads that are more than ¼ in. wide. That's because the bigger the bead, the longer it takes to cure. However, if time isn't a problem, a larger bead won't be a problem.

I always start at an inside corner. If there is an inside corner at each end of a joint,

**Get rid of the old caulk first.** A good, flexible utility knife, such as this one that has break-off blades, can reach down behind the old caulk to cut it loose from the surface. Remember to take care when cutting near a fixture that's made of fiberglass or another soft material.

**Start the bead at an inside corner.** By starting at each corner and overlapping in the middle, you can keep a watchful eye on the bead as it comes out of the caulk gun and carefully control the pressure on the bead.

It's critical to the job to keep the caulk flowing smoothly and not to let it squeeze out from either side. With practice, anyone can lay a long, even bead.

then I work out from both, joining the two beads somewhere in the middle. Otherwise, if I caulk continuously from one inside corner to the next, I end up obstructing my own view of the bead and risk putting a kink in the bead at the point where I turn the gun toward the other corner.

If there is a three-legged joint, such as where two tub-enclosure walls meet the tub, I do the vertical joint first. I keep the caulk flowing smoothly out under the angled tip and am careful not to let it squeeze out from either side. It takes some practice to lay down a long, even bead, especially to be able to slow down just enough to compensate for the reduced flow when releasing the trigger to start another stroke.

Some manufacturers recommend pushing the gun away from you as you lay down caulk, but I like to pull the gun away from the bead. Pushing the gun won't squeeze the caulk down into a gap as well as having the long angled tip bearing against the bead as you move along. Also, pushing the gun obscures the bead, which makes it impossible to control its size and position.

## The Best Bead Tool Is Always within Reach

I almost always tool each bead immediately after applying it before I move to the next joint. This way, I'm sure I get to the material before it skins over. Also, if I have to add a bit more on top somewhere, I want to do this while it's in its most workable state.

Like a lot of people, I find that the most useful tool for dressing joints is a finger, which can adapt itself to the small variations in the surface or size of the joint. If I've put down a bead that is no larger than necessary, one firm swipe with my finger usually gives a nice convex shape to the joint and adheres it firmly to the surfaces on both sides of the gap or angle.

Small irregularities in the caulk will trap dirt and harbor mildew, making for unsightly problems later on. For this reason, I take more care than would be needed just to ensure a watertight joint. Most times, I wet my finger with saliva and go over the joint again, polishing it and eliminating tiny irregularities. I've tried wetting my finger with water, but saliva seems to work best. I'm careful not to wet the ends of a bead where the next bead needs to adhere to it.

I talked to several manufacturers of silicone caulk, none of whom recommend a licked finger to tool their caulk. All agree, however, that the licked finger is in widespread use and that there is no major health risk involved. They also say it's not a good idea to allow silicone to stay on the skin. They recommend using a spoon dipped in soapy water or smeared with petroleum jelly. I haven't had a problem doing it my way, though. But silicone isn't particularly tasty, so I keep paper towels or newspapers handy to clean my finger.

Sometimes, usually when a joint is wider than my finger can bridge properly, I need a different tool. I keep an old cereal spoon with a fairly tight radius on the tip just for

Usually, a firm, even swipe of the finger gives just the right convex shape to a caulk joint. The author's preferred lubricant for his finger is saliva, but he's careful to wipe off his finger before putting it back in his mouth.

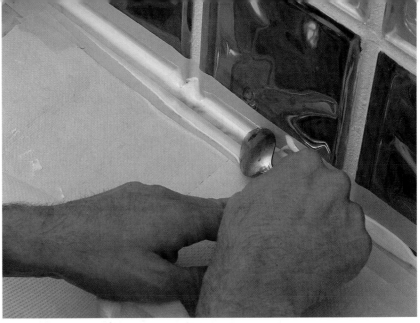

A spoon that has a fairly tight radius on the tip can create just about any type of cross section, even a wide joint such as the one around this glass-block window. Sometimes it's necessary to mask around the bead with tape.

this purpose. Turning the spoon at various angles, I can create just about any type of cross section I need.

I find that the spoon works best used in a scooping position instead of with its rounded back pressed into the bead (photo above right). When tooling with the spoon, I do a dry run along the joint before applying the caulk, testing for the proper angle to achieve the bead I want.

# Finishing Up and Putting Away the Caulk

When I'm tooling a wider joint using the spoon—a joint that's ¼ in. wide or more—it's often impossible not to have some caulk squeeze out on both sides of the tool. I don't worry about this. The hard edges of the spoon create a definite edge to the joint and scrape a clean track right beside it. If I go back an hour or two later, when the caulk has just firmed up, I can scrape away the excess.

I rarely mask both sides of a joint with tape; I don't like to because the edge of the bead cannot feather down to absolutely nothing due to the thickness of the masking tape.

I've heard many tips about how to close spouts of partially used tubes of caulking, but generally they don't help for long.

After you snip the tip of the caulk nozzle, save the little cone of plastic. When you're ready to seal the tube, squeeze a little caulking out the tip and press the inverted tip back into the hole for a snug fit.

Any seal has to be airtight. Some manufacturers help by supplying snap-on caps for spouts, but even this solution doesn't work if you've had to cut the spout short to get a wide bead. I save the tip I cut off when I started the tube. Inverting this into the opening and holding it in place with a bit of caulk squeezed out around the edges works better than anything else I've tried (bottom photo).

*Brian Zavitz is a renovation contractor in Toronto, Ontario, Canada.*

# A Look at Bathroom Lighting

■ BY ANDREW WORMER

The upstairs bathroom of my condo has terrible lighting. No matter how sunny a morning it is, I shower in gloom. And when I stand in front of the sink to brush my teeth and comb my hair, I'm always surprised by all the new wrinkles and dark shadows that have magically appeared on my face overnight.

Although the view in my mirror is sobering enough, even more sobering is the fact that the lighting in this bathroom isn't unusual. Countless bathrooms across the country have similar lighting: a combo ventilation fan/light fixture located approximately in the middle of the 5-ft. by 8-ft. ceiling and another recessed fixture over the sink. This kind of lighting is guaranteed to make you look bad, whether you're the designer of the bathroom, the builder, or the person using it. Fortunately, coming up with a better lighting plan isn't difficult. To choose the right bathroom-lighting fixtures, first you have to focus on the object you want to illuminate.

## Begin with the Vanity

In my bathroom, the task lighting (see Glossary, p. 130) is supplied by a single recessed fixture. It contains a 50w R20 incandescent reflector lamp—also known as a light bulb. This is a bad idea. The narrowly focused light from this fixture does a good job of lighting the sink, but it's supposed to light my face. Instead, it shines directly on top of my head, casting weird shadows under my eyes, cheekbones, and chin.

Lots of people like recessed fixtures, which are also called recessed cans. They're versatile and unobtrusive and can provide both narrowly focused or broadly diffused light. But one thing that they don't do well is provide good vanity lighting. If you insist on using recessed-can fixtures for this purpose, be sure to use more than one, and offset them to both sides of the sink. Multiple recessed fixtures will help to soften shadows and supply a more diffuse light.

**A combination is best.** This windowless bathroom has a skylight to admit daylight. The incandescent tube lights (Alinea® by Aamsco) flank the lavatory, creating even illumination at the counter.

# A Glossary of Bathroom-Lighting Guidelines and Terminology

**GENERAL LIGHT**
Ceiling-mounted fixtures supply general lighting. They should always be accompanied by task lighting.

**NATURAL LIGHT**
Windows and skylights are good sources of light and ventilation. When possible, they should equal at least 10 percent of the floor area of the bathroom.

**DECORATIVE LIGHT**
Wall-mounted sconces are a decorative source of indirect light.

**WET LOCATION LIGHTS**
Fixtures over baths or showers should be vaporproof, such as this recessed-can fixture.

**TASK LIGHTING**
Task lighting at the vanity is best accomplished by two fixtures mounted at eye level to provide vertical cross illumination.

**GENERAL LIGHTING**
in the form of wall or ceiling-mounted fixtures or recessed-can fixtures is required in larger bathrooms. For ceiling-mounted fixtures, plan on about 1w of incandescent light per square foot of floor area. Recessed-light fixtures need at least twice that wattage to achieve the same amount of illumination, while fluorescent fixtures require about one-third to one-half the amount of wattage of incandescent fixtures. Dark surfaces require more wattage than bathrooms with light-colored walls.

**TASK LIGHTING**
is generally located near the vanity area, but is sometimes a bathroom's general-lighting source as well, particularly in small rooms.

**ACCENT LIGHTING**
emphasizes an object or surface, but not itself. Placed in a cabinet toe kick, for example, accent lighting can make the vanity appear to float.

**DECORATIVE LIGHTING**
places the emphasis on the style of the light fixture, while simultaneously providing some indirect light.

The goal of any type of vanity lighting is not to light the mirror, the sink, or the top of the head, but to light the face. Therefore, the best vanity task lighting is supplied by wall-mounted fixtures at eye level on both sides of the mirror. When these types of fixtures have multiple lamps that are arranged vertically, they produce desirable, virtually shadowless lighting that is called vertical cross illumination.

## VERTICAL LIGHTS ARE THE MOST FLATTERING

Many different types of fixtures produce this type of lighting. For example, most folks are familiar with so-called "Hollywood lights," or metal strips with multiple incandescent globe lamps. My downstairs bathroom has a single Hollywood light mounted above the mirror, and the light quality is much better than in the upstairs bath. This simple theatrical design has mutated into many different consumer-oriented incarnations, but the original idea was to surround a mirror with light that would shine evenly onto the face. Of course, most residential bathrooms forget about the lights on the side and simply mount a single light strip above the mirror. This option produces mirror lighting better than that of most ceiling-mounted fixtures but still not as good as fixtures mounted to the sides of the mirror.

## ALTERNATIVES TO HOLLYWOOD LIGHTS

Besides Hollywood lights, other types of fixtures can be mounted at or near eye level on both sides of the mirror as well. Wall-mounted sconces, brackets, and diffusers are available in a wide range of designs and in every style imaginable. The best ones all have this trait in common: You can't look directly at the lamps because they are shielded in some way by translucent lenses or by the position of the fixture. If you choose Hollywood lights, which have exposed lamps, you should use frosted lamps rather than clear ones to reduce glare.

Linear lamps—tubes of various lengths and diameters—are available in both incandescent and fluorescent varieties. They are an increasingly popular alternative to Hollywood lights, especially now that fluorescent lamps have advanced beyond their flickering and buzzing early days. Some designers use fluorescent tube lights in creative ways that make one-of-a-kind fixtures, such as the vanity lighting by architects Steven and Cathi House (photo right).

## Light from Both Sides Is Best

A face lighted by an overhead light will have sharply accentuated shadows. Flanking the mirror with a row of vertical lights, however, creates even illumination that eliminates shadows.

*The best vanity task lighting is supplied by wall-mounted fixtures at eye level on both sides of the mirror.*

Glass blocks can be light fixtures, too. A pair of linear fluorescent lamps mounted behind this mirror bounce their light off a wall of glass block. The back of the mirror, which is held 4 in. off the block, is painted white to reflect the light better.

Natural daylight is considered the benchmark against which artificial light is compared. But even natural light varies in appearance, ranging from the warm reddish light of the setting sun to the clear blue light of a northern sky.

Color temperature is an objective measurement (in degrees Kelvin) of a light source's appearance. The higher the color temperature, the cooler the light source appears. Late-afternoon sun has a color temperature of about 4000°K, while a brilliant blue sky has a color temperature of about 8500°K.

Incandescent lamps produce light that has a color temperature of about 2800°K, a temperature considered warm and inviting. Normal fluorescent lamps have a cooler light in the 4000°K to 5000°K range, which is perceived as being harsh and unfriendly, or bright and alert depending on your point of view.

Skin tones are best rendered by lamps with a color temperature in the warm range, or 2800°K to 3500°K, and with a high (80+) color rendering index (CRI), a measurement of a light source's ability to render color accurately.

### A COMPARISON OF DIFFERENT TYPES OF LIGHT SOURCES

| Lamp description | Watts* | Lumens (brightness) | Life** | °Kelvin | Annual cost*** |
|---|---|---|---|---|---|
| A Incandescent globe | 25 | 210 | 1,500 | 2550 | $ 3.75 |
| B Incandescent "A" | 60 | 870 | 1,000 | 2800 | $ 9.00 |
| C Halogen minican | 75 | 1,200 | 2,000 | 3000 | $11.25 |
| D Fluorescent compact twin | 13 | 825 | 10,000 | 2700 | $ 2.10 |
| E Fluorescent compact quad | 26 | 1,800 | 10,000 | 2700 | $ 4.80 |
| F Fluorescent tube (1 in. by 48 in.) | 32 | 3,050 | 20,000 | 3000 | $ 5.40 |

\* Includes ballast wattage for fluorescents
\*\* Average number of hours a light source is expected to burn
\*\*\* Calculated at 10¢ per kwh based on average residential use of 1,500 hours per year (includes ballast wattage)
(Chart courtesy American Lighting Association)

Despite the improvements to fluorescent lighting, however, some skeptics are still convinced that they need incandescent lighting in the bathroom. Want an incandescent lamp in a tube? Alkco® Lighting's Lincandescent fixture is a good choice for vanity lighting because of its sleek design and diffuse, warm light.

## Don't Forget the Tub and Shower

Building codes wisely discourage the use of lighting fixtures that can be easily reached while standing in a shower or sitting in a tub. This restriction means that track lighting and cord-connected hanging fixtures can't be located within 8 ft. vertically and

3 ft. horizontally of the rim of a bathtub [NEC 410-4(d)]. In addition, fixtures used in wet locations (like a shower) need to be certified specifically for this use. Over the years, I've seen some interesting interpretations of these rules, but practically speaking, this rule means that vaporproof ceiling-mounted or recessed-can fixtures are needed here.

Don't make the mistake (like the builder of my condominium did) of assuming that a combo fan/light mounted in the middle of an average-size bathroom will supply enough light to a tub/shower area. Glass shower doors don't block much light, but many kinds of opaque shower curtains do, leaving the occupant in the dark when the curtains are drawn. A vapor-rated fixture centrally located over the shower or tub is the best solution. Keep in mind, however, that a bright overhead light may not create the right ambience for a long soak in a tub. That's why it isn't a bad idea to put this light on a dimmer control. Russ Leslie, director of the Lighting Research Center at Rensselaer Polytechnic Institute[SM], suggests that a shower light can also double as night-lighting because it probably doesn't bathe the bath in bright light. For that reason, the switch should be located near the entryway.

If you do opt for the combination light/ventilation fan, don't make the mistake of skimping on quality. Ultraquiet low-noise (less than 1.5 sones) fans that are barely audible are worth the extra money. Loud fans are so irritating that they often go unused.

## Have Adequate General Lighting

As bathrooms have become larger, there has been a parallel increase in demand for general and decorative lighting. Architect Joe Rey-Barreau particularly likes wall sconces as a more attractive alternative to typical overhead lighting. He also noted that he is seeing more suspended decorative fixtures in

General lighting is supplied by both the skylight and the recessed-can fixtures overhead, while wall-mounted fixtures supply important task lighting for the vanity.

**Rope lights make good accents.** Tiny incandescent lights bound into a flexible PVC tube can be snaked behind valances.

A problem with recessed-can fixtures is that they can make your ceiling look and act like Swiss cheese. The appearance factor is manageable: just don't use more recessed lights than you really need. The larger issue is air infiltration. Moist bathroom air pouring through the holes in a bathroom ceiling can condense in an attic, creating potential for mold, mildew, or structural damage.

One solution that I've found to this problem is Juno® Lighting's Air-Loc® IC fixture. This recessed can has an unperforated housing to stop air leaks, and it comes with peel-and-stick gaskets to prevent leaks around the rim of the fixture. I also like Juno's comprehensive range of baffles, diffusers, reflectors, and louvers that fit in their mounting frames.

## Decorative Lighting

As you can see, general lighting can also double as decorative lighting. One concept of Rey-Barreau's that I think is helpful in planning bathroom lighting is to think in terms of "layers of light." One layer is the lighting in the vanity area, which in some small powder rooms may be enough. If a bathroom is larger or if it has separate compartments for the toilet, tub, or sink, it will need another layer to light these areas. Some bathrooms might even need a third layer of light, consisting of wall sconces, recessed-can fixtures, or other ceiling-mounted fixtures to supplement the light of the other two layers. The fourth layer—decorative lighting—is primarily for effect.

Lighting layers can overlap. General lighting can be supplied by an architectural valance, soffit, or cove, for example, particularly in high-ceilinged rooms. Linear fluorescent lamps are ideal for this application because of their cool temperature, long life (they don't need to be changed often), energy efficiency (the lights can be left on), and the diffuse light they produce.

Some designers like to use decorative lighting in unusual places—in the toekick

**TIP**

*A bright overhead light may not create the right ambience for a long soak in a tub. Consider putting this light on a dimmer control.*

bathrooms now, such as chandeliers and suspended uplights and downlights.

In some situations, you don't want the fixture to be a decorative element. All you really want is the light it provides. In this case, recessed lights really shine. Recessed-can fixtures are available in different sizes, shapes, and styles, and they accept incandescent, halogen, and compact fluorescent lamps. Their placement in the ceiling depends on their purpose. Downlights should be above task areas, but offset slightly to minimize glare and shadows. Downlights mounted near a wall create a scalloped effect and accentuate the wall's texture: a good idea when you have a finely crafted brick wall, a bad idea when the light shines on a poorly taped gypsum wall.

There are too many manufacturers of recessed-can fixtures to list here, but better ones share these traits: They have interchangeable reflector and trim options, and they are available in IC-rated (insulated ceiling) mounting frames for fixtures to be in second-story or attic locations. An IC-recessed can has a shield to keep it from overheating when it's under a blanket of insulation.

area of a cabinet, for instance, or inside a cabinet with glass doors. Low-voltage (12v or 24v) halogen lighting is well suited for this purpose. Small halogen lamps produce a lot of light for their size and can be placed in a number of different kinds of fixtures depending on the application. Remember that all low-voltage lighting needs a transformer.

Another option is decorative rope lighting. This snakey stuff is a supple ½-in.-dia. PVC tube with tiny bulbs at 1-in. intervals. At $3.50 to $12 per ft., it isn't expensive, and it can be placed in unusual locations for unexpected accents. Rope lighting is available in different colors. It can be cut at designated intervals (typically 18 in.), and it can be bent and twisted to replicate the look of neon lights. Both low-voltage and line-voltage rope lighting is available at specialty lighting shops or via the Internet.

# Where Should I Shop for Fixtures?

In researching this article, I pressed industry professionals for advice on choosing specific fixtures and then finding suppliers. The rule is that there aren't any rules. For some designers, the key issues (besides the actual quality of the fixture itself) were service and availability. Other designers pointed out that all the new lamps and technology have vastly expanded the range of fixtures now available. New innovations—for example, compact-fluorescent lamps that are now the same size as incandescents, tiny T-4 halogen lamps, narrow-diameter T-5 linear fluorescent lamps—really drive the latest fixture designs. And now we have the Internet to fuel our searches.

Although designers mentioned such things as UL-listing, plastic vs. metal holders and glass vs. plastic lenses, they all seemed to agree that the real story was not so much the fixture (although style and quality are important) but the lamp that the fixture

## Sources

**Aamsco Lighting**
100 Lamp Light Circle
Summerville,
SC 29483
(800) 221-9092
www.aamsco.com

**Alkco Lighting**
11500 Melrose Ave.
Franklin Park,
IL 60131
(847) 451-0700
www.alkco.com

**American Lighting Association**
P.O. Box 420288
Dallas, TX 75342
(800) 274-4484
www.americanlighting-assoc.com

**Brass Light Gallery**
P.O. Box 674
Milwaukee, WI 53201
(800) 243-9595
www.brasslight.com

**Cooper Industries Corporate Office**
600 Travis,
Suite 5800
Houston, TX 77002
(713) 209-8400
www.cooper-lighting.com

**Energy Federation Inc.**
401 Washington St.,
Suite 3000
Westborough,
MA 01581
(800) 876-0660
www.efi.org

**Hesco Lighting**
71 Beaver Ave.
Clinton, NJ 08809
(888) 367-7946
www.hesco-lighting.com

**Juno Lighting**
1300 S. Wolf Rd.
P.O. Box 5065
Des Plaines, IL 60017
(847) 827-9880
www.junolighting.com

**Lamps Plus**
20250 Plummer St.
Chatsworth,
CA 91311
(800) 782-1967
www.lampsplus.com

**Lighting Paradise Corporation**
5455 S.W. 8th St.
Miami, FL 33134
(877) 544-4863
www.lighting-paradise.com

**Lucid Lighting**
287 S. Main St.
Lambertville,
NJ 08530
(609) 397-9581
www.lucidlighting.com

**Philips Lighting**
200 Franklin
Square Dr.
Somerset, NJ 08875
(800) 805-2517
www.lighting.-philips.com

**Rejuvenation**
2550 NW Nicolai St.
Portland, OR 97210
(888) 401-1900
www.rejuvenation.com

**Sea Gull Lighting**
3000 Cindel Dr.
Cinnaminson,
NJ 08077
(800) 347-5483
www.seagull-lighting.com

holds and the quality of light that it produces. Decide what it is you want to light, choose the lamp that does the best job, and then figure out which fixture will hold that lamp.

*Andrew Wormer is a contributing editor for* Fine Homebuilding *magazine and the author of* The Builder's Book of Bathrooms *(The Taunton Press, 1998) and* The Bathroom Idea Book *(The Taunton Press, 1999).*

# Choosing and Installing a Bathroom-Vent Fan

■ BY REX CAULDWELL

I once received a call from a homeowner complaining that his bathroom fan was not working. Although I responded within a few hours, I was too late to save the fan and far too late to save the bathroom. The room was victim to moisture damage from humid air: The wallpaper had begun to peel, and the drywall was blackened around the shower. It was obvious this fan had not worked in a long time. As the homeowner witnessed, moisture-laden air over time can cause a lot of damage in a bathroom, such as corroded light fixtures, rotted wood, and peeling wallpaper and paint. Moisture can also hasten the spread of unhealthful mold and mildew. A properly operating fan removes moisture-laden air from the bathroom and replaces it with dry air from outside the room.

Most building codes require fans in bathrooms that have no windows. But fans should be installed in all bathrooms, window or not, especially in cold climates (it's ludicrous to think a person would open a window to ventilate the room when it's freezing outside). There are many types of bathroom fans out there, and the choice may seem simple: choosing the unit with the best price. But remember that the best price is not always the cheapest price—you get what you pay for.

## Choose a Fan that Moves a Sufficient Amount of Air

First consider the size of the bathroom, and then choose a fan large enough to move air adequately for that size room. The volume of air the fan moves is measured in cubic feet per minute (cfm) and will be listed on the unit. To choose the fan with the correct cfm rating for the room size, first figure the volume of air in the bathroom and then

Metal hangers locate the fan box at the proper height and allow some flexibility in fan positioning.

*A properly operating fan removes moisture-laden air from the bathroom and replaces it with dry air from outside the room.*

divide that number by 7.5, per guidelines of the Home Ventilating Institute (a division of the Air Movement and Control Association International Inc.). Assuming 8-ft. ceilings, you typically would choose a 50-cfm unit for a small bathroom (around 5 ft. by 8 ft.), an 80-cfm unit for a midsize bathroom (around 8 ft. by 8 ft.) and a 110-cfm unit for a large bathroom (around 10 ft. by 10 ft.). For larger bathrooms, companies such as Panasonic make 190-cfm fans.

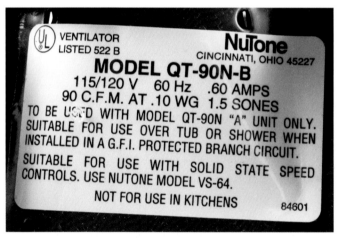

Every fan has its cubic feet/minute (cfm) airflow and noise ratings (measured in sones) listed on the motor housing. The lower the sone rating, the quieter the fan. However, the noise ratings usually rise as the cfm rating increases.

## Quiet Fans Are Better Fans

In general, the higher the cfm rating a fan has, the more noise it makes. But the noise doesn't have to shake the floor. You should choose the quietest unit for the amount of air that must be moved. A fan's noise is measured in sones, and each unit should have this measurement clearly labeled on the box or in the product literature. A noisy fan is one that's rated above 3 sones. You'll be able to hear a fan this loud even while the shower is running (it will sound like a helicopter landing on your roof). A quiet fan, on the other hand, measures around 2 sones to 3 sones. An ultraquiet fan will be 1 sone or less.

## Combination Units Should Be Heat Resistant

It's common for manufacturers to sell fan units combined with lights or heaters or both. However, these units come with inherent problems. Because of the heat generated by incandescent bulbs, ceiling fixtures are often limited to lower-watt bulbs, which do not provide abundant illumination. This

# When Venting a Bathroom Fan, Keep the Run Short and Smooth

A common error in bathroom-fan installations is venting the fan into the attic. Sending moist air into attic spaces could damage wood members and insulation, so you must vent the fan outside, which means running ductwork.

There are several types of duct available: rigid (metal, PVC) and flexible (insulated, noninsulated) vinyl pipe. The two types of rigid duct, metal and schedule-20 (thin-wall) PVC are the best because they have smooth inner walls that don't impede airflow. The rigid types are more time-consuming to install (each turn in direction requires a separate fitting) but have better seals and last longer. Flexible pipe is the easiest to install but has greater air resistance because of the accordionlike folds of the pipe wall. If you choose flexible duct, it's best to use the wider 6-in. dia. pipe; the larger diameter will offset decreased airflow. Both types of rigid duct, as well as the flexible kind, can be found at your local home center. Whatever type of duct is used, be sure to seal the joints properly. Remember that in unheated spaces, ducting must be insulated to reduce condensation.

## Running duct

For the most efficient airflow, try to run the duct in a straight line to the exterior, pitching the duct down at a slight angle to the outside wall so that condensation will drain out and not back into the fan. For every significant bend, you slow airflow; gradual turns are better than right-angle ones. In my experience, if you have more than four significant turns, you may have to increase the cfm of the fan to provide sufficient air movement.

**Rigid-PVC ductwork decreases air resistance. Although more labor intensive to install, rigid ductwork has smooth inner walls that don't impede airflow.**

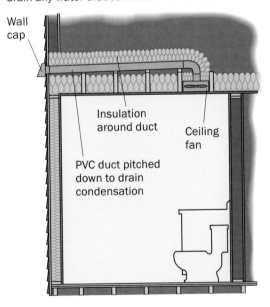

**DUCTING A BATH FAN**
The best way to increase airflow is to reduce the amount of air resistance in the ducting. Ideally, the run of the duct should be short, straight, and pitched slightly to the outside to drain any water that condenses in the duct.

Wall cap

Insulation around duct

Ceiling fan

PVC duct pitched down to drain condensation

heat, along with the bulb's ultraviolet (UV) rays, may degrade cheap-plastic light covers, turning them an unsightly brown. To combat this, either get a fan/light with a glass cover (preferred) or a UV-resistant plastic cover. I recommend that you install a fan-only unit and install a separate light.

Fans with heaters are popular, but I don't like them. The fan will suck heated air outside, defeating the purpose of the heater. I prefer wall-mounted, fan-operated heaters with thermostats. These types of units can also keep plumbing from freezing.

## Installing the Fan

The first installation step is choosing a location for the fan. It should be installed as close as possible to the shower without actually being in the shower, unless it is rated for wet locations. Any fan within arm's reach of the shower should be protected by a ground-fault circuit interrupter. Typically, the fan unit is mounted between the ceiling joists, a determining factor in the fan's position.

Some units require you to remove the fan module from its housing before mounting (photo above). To do this, loosen the bottom screws and pull out the fan assembly. In one corner of the box, you will see a splice box that the fan plugs into; remove the splice box, too.

In new ceiling installations, the instructions say simply to attach the unit's arms to the ceiling joist, allowing just enough of the fan to hang below the joist for the drywall to fit within the lip of the fan's frame (top photo, p. 137). I normally throw the arms away and screw the fan directly to the joist: It's much more secure that way, as well as faster and simpler. If you're installing your own drywall, you will immediately note a problem: How in the heck do you get the drywall into the lipped frame? Well, you don't. You have to cut the drywall carefully to fit around the fan. You can install the drywall first, cut the hole exactly, and then insert the fan. But here is another way: Cut

To gain access to the splice box, remove the fan from the fan housing. After loosening the two bottom screws on the housing, slide the fan out. Usually tucked into the box's corner, the splice box can be opened with a nut driver.

the drywall (the entire sheet) to stop at the joist the fan is attached to, cut a U-shape into the next sheet and insert it under the fan's lip. Fans do not have to be mounted only in the ceiling; they also can be placed in a wall. If the wall is exterior, it makes for a fast duct run.

## Wiring the Fan

It's best to bring the power to the switch first and then to the fan. That makes it easier to troubleshoot the circuit. Use a screwdriver to remove the knockout on the fan's splice box (left photo, p. 141). Remove the splice-box cover, insert a nonmetallic (NM) connector into the knockout, and screw on the nut (right photo, p. 141). Don't just bring the cable in through the sharp bare metal hole; vibration will cause a sharp edge to cut through the cable insulation. Bring in 6 in. of cable (trim as necessary), strip the cable's sheathing to within

*The fan should be installed as close as possible to the shower without actually being in the shower, unless it is rated for wet locations.*

# Wiring Diagrams for Switches and Fan Units

When you're installing a bath fan, each function of the fan unit is usually assigned a switch; you don't want the heater to start each time you turn the light on. Also, remember that code does not allow you to connect the fan circuit to a bathroom-receptacle circuit.

### WIRING A SINGLE-POLE SWITCH TO A FAN

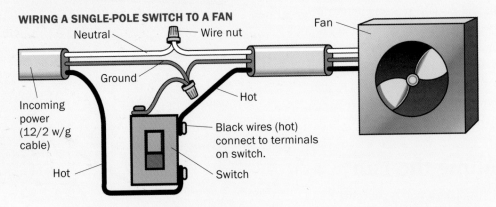

Neutral — Wire nut

Fan

Ground

Hot

Incoming power (12/2 w/g cable)

Black wires (hot) connect to terminals on switch.

Hot

Switch

### WIRING A SWITCH FOR A FAN/LIGHT COMBINATION

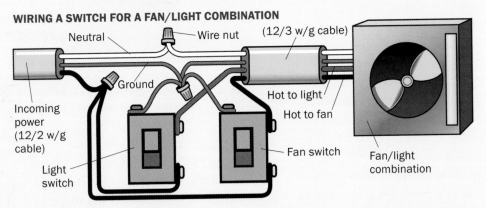

Neutral — Wire nut

(12/3 w/g cable)

Ground

Hot to light

Hot to fan

Incoming power (12/2 w/g cable)

Light switch

Fan switch

Fan/light combination

### WIRING A SWITCH FOR A FAN/LIGHT/HEATER COMBINATION

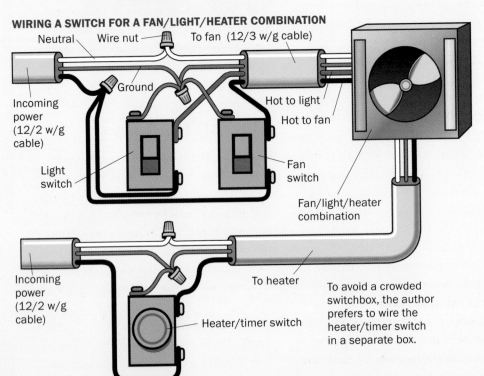

Neutral — Wire nut — To fan (12/3 w/g cable)

Ground

Hot to light

Hot to fan

Incoming power (12/2 w/g cable)

Light switch

Fan switch

Fan/light/heater combination

Incoming power (12/2 w/g cable)

To heater

Heater/timer switch

To avoid a crowded switchbox, the author prefers to wire the heater/timer switch in a separate box.

Remove the knockout with a screwdriver. Locate the nearest knockout to the incoming wires, insert a screwdriver into the slot, and wiggle the knockout loose.

NM connector keeps the wire's insulation from getting cut. After threading the NM connector into the knockout hole, slide the cable into the fan box and tighten the connector's screws.

¼ in. of the housing, and in a simple installation, connect black to black and white to white. Don't forget to attach the bare ground wire to the metal box.

If you have a fan/light combo and if you want the fan and light to be on at different times, you will need two hot feeds and one white neutral return. Use three-way switch cable (black, red, white, and bare ground). If you also have a night-light in the combo, you will need three-way cable for the fan/light and another cable (12/2 or 14/2 with ground) to feed the night-light. If you also have a heater, you'll need to run two three-way cables into the housing. With all these cables, you must make a neat splice within the combo's splice box, or there won't be enough room for all the wires to fold back in.

## Wiring the Switches

You have two basic wiring options. The first is to bring the power feed into the fan splice box; I don't recommend that you do this because the box is too crowded already. The second option is bringing the power feed to the switch. Wire the neutrals together, and bring the black wires to the switch. There are three general choices for bathroom fans: standard switches, dimmers, and timers. You'll need a large-volume box (at least 30 cu. in.) to fit all the wires to the multitude of switches. Many manufacturers make a special switch for combination units; it's a pair or trio of switches that fits in the space normally occupied by one. These switches are meant for a single gang box, and there may not be enough room to squeeze all the wires in. However, you can get a special cover that converts a large square box with screws on its corners to a single. This gives you lots of splicing room. Remember not to power the fan from the bath receptacle. The bath receptacle must have its own 20-amp circuit. Power the fan or fan/light from a living room or bedroom circuit. If you have a heater in the fan, bring in a separate circuit for the fixture.

*Rex Cauldwell is a master electrician/plumber living in Virginia. He is the author of* Wiring a House, Safe Home Wiring Projects, *and* Inspecting a House, *all published by The Taunton Press.*

## Sources

**Air Movement and Control Association (AMCA)**
30 West University Dr.
Arlington Heights,
IL 60004
(847) 394-0150
www.amca.org

# What's Hot in Bathroom Heaters?

■ BY DAVID ERICSON

I have a vivid childhood memory of standing at our bathroom sink with an exposed electric-coil heater humming on the wall to the left of my head, crackling as dust hit the element. It was like standing in a toaster whose burners worked on only one side. I didn't want to go too far from that heater on a winter morning, though, because the window on the other side of the bathroom might have an interior coat of ice. We didn't bother trying to bathe in that room.

At the other end of the rainbow, a bathroom might have a fireplace, a whirlpool, radiant floors, hydronic tubing behind the mirrors to prevent fogging, and his and hers towel warmers—Myson® offers a gold-plated model for $7,000. Somewhere between these two extremes, there are lots of options for people who need a little extra heat when they step out of the tub or shower.

This is an introduction to bathroom-heating options. Choosing among them depends a lot on specific circumstances at the work site: physical layout of the building, budget, and the contractor's experience. Of course, extra bathroom heat is best

planned when the home's heating system is laid in, but that planning does not always happen. Some of the systems described here are specifically designed for bathroom additions or remodels, so you don't necessarily have to overhaul your furnace to get the heat that you need.

## Before Adding More Heat, Save the Heat You've Got

If you're upgrading the heating system in an existing bath, begin by calculating how much heat the room loses through underinsulation and air leaks around windows, doors, outlets, switches, and recessed lighting. You can hire an HVAC contractor to pinpoint your heat loss precisely. Or you can do a lot with common sense. Bathroom air is often warmer than air elsewhere in the house, creating a pressure difference that results in warm air actively seeking a way out of the bathroom. Just stopping drafts makes a huge difference, even if the temperature stays the same. Reducing heat loss by

## Rules of Thumb for Sizing Bathroom Heaters

Andrew Wormer's *The Builder's Book of Bathrooms* (The Taunton Press, 1998) recommends keeping an occupied bathroom's temperature 5°F above the ambient temperature of the rest of the house. Having the bathroom be a separate heating zone makes it easy to achieve this difference without overheating the rest of the house. Because bathrooms are small spaces and because running a bath or shower generates a fair amount of heat already, the extra couple of degrees should not require much energy to provide.

There are various quantitative measures by which to estimate need. But none of these rules of thumb takes into account nonstandard ceiling heights or heat-loss calculations for your particular space. John Siegenthaler, author of *Modern Hydronic Heating: Residential* (DelMar Publishing,

1995), reports that an average bathroom heat load is 4000 British thermal units per hour (Btu/h) to 8000 Btu/h, but that large custom bathrooms may need more. Runtal, a manufacturer of radiant wall panels and towel warmers, advises planning on roughly "40 Btu/h per sq. ft. of floor area, assuming a single outside window and a standard ceiling height." For electric heaters rated by wattage, one rule of thumb is to multiply square footage by 10 in a mild climate or by 15 in a more severe climate. According to this formula, a 100-sq.-ft. bathroom would need a 1000w–1500w heater.

Ray Farley of Myson uses another equation, estimating Btu/h output based on a heater's wattage. Farley reports that 1000w equals roughly 3400 Btu/h. According to Runtal's 40-Btu per sq. ft. rule, that would heat 85 sq. ft.

sealing air leaks, improving insulation, and upgrading windows will reduce the active heating requirement considerably. This backstage work makes possible an elegant heating system, one that does the job simply, without occupying much space or using much energy. Now you're ready to calculate just how much heat you really need.

## The Simplest Solutions Are Stand-Alone Heaters

Heat lamps, ceiling fixtures, wall units, and tiny electric heaters that fit in the cabinet kick space are all worth considering. Infrared heating lamps are the least effective of the bunch. They are meant only to heat the skin when you're stepping out of the bath. They tend to warm only what is within a few inches of them—the food at a restaurant buffet table, or your head and shoulders in the bathroom. They are inexpensive, easy to install, and, in the right situation, just fine. One of those heating units was more than sufficient where I stayed recently in Florida.

Similarly inexpensive and easy to install, baseboard heaters use the principle that hot air rises to warm the entire room. Air heats as it passes over either heating fins or hydronic tubes, the heated air rises, and cooler air near the floor repeats the cycle until the air in the room reaches the temperature called for by the thermostat. Baseboards require two things: that you have sufficient linear wall space and that you want to use your linear wall space in that way.

Low price is the only advantage of electric baseboards. Landlords like them because they are inexpensive to buy and install, and the tenant pays the electricity bill. If the house has hydronic baseboards elsewhere,

# Quick Fixes Might Be Enough

Stand-alone heaters offer relatively low cost and easy installation. Electric units such as those shown here by NuTone require only an extra electrical cable.

Overhead, infrared heat lamps and ceiling-mounted forced-air units will take off some of the chill. Heat lamps (1) provide spot heat as you step out of the shower. For small spaces with basic needs, NuTone makes an overhead unit (2) that has a 100w light bulb in the center, a 70-cfm vent fan on one side and a 1500w, 5118-Btu forced-air heater on the other. This no-frills unit is inexpensive but noisy.

If you rely on forced air to distribute heat, it might make more sense to use a wall unit and dedicate the ceiling to lights and ventilation. A wall unit (3) will accelerate convection and can heat the whole room for less than $200. Many electric heaters now come field-convertible for a choice of voltages and wattages. Kick-space heaters offer floor-level forced air without occupying the linear wall space that baseboard heaters do, and can be electric (4) or hydronic (5). This hydronic model by VRV Products can tie into an existing hydronic system without a major renovation.

one more in the bathroom makes perfect sense and is energy efficient. Metal baseboards are prone to corrosion in high-humidity situations, however, so be sure to specify a corrosion-resistant paint, such as the paint on Slant/Fin's® Rust Resistor model.

Small forced-air kick-space heaters or wall units don't require the linear wall space of baseboard heaters. Kick-space heaters fit into the base of cabinets or slip into the wall between studs. VRV Products' Quiet One® 2000 kick-space heater is a hydronic unit whose fan uses about the same amount of electricity as a 40w bulb to disperse heat. This option makes sense if a house has a hydronic system elsewhere but you either can't or would rather not tear up the bathroom floor to add a radiant floor. NuTone makes all-electric kick-space and wall units that are field-adaptable to switch between 120v and 240v, and range between 500w and 1500w (1500w is the maximum allowable at 120v). Blowing hot air across the floor, the fans can heat it enough to make an island of warmth if the floor is otherwise cold. The list prices for these models of heaters run between $113 and $190, plus installation.

A caution: If you choose an electric wall heater, make sure that it isn't installed below a towel bar or within the swing of a door that may include a towel or coat hook. A garment or towel draped over an electric-resistance heater can easily catch fire.

# Radiant Heat Offers Efficient, Draft-Free Comfort

People use the words "radiant heat" to refer to both hydronic and electric systems. Most radiant systems work by the gentle convection of a thermal mass, such as a heated floor, and by radiating varying amounts of infrared energy. For example, hydronic tubing heats a floor through conduction to a relatively low temperature, 85°F being about the warmest floor that is still comfortable. Then the thermal mass of the floor—besides feeling great on your feet—heats the air slightly through gradual convection. But some percentage of energy escapes the floor as infrared-energy waves that people and solid surfaces absorb and convert to heat.

John Siegenthaler of Appropriate Designs, an engineering firm in Holland Patent, New York, says that "low-temperature radiant floors are typically about one-third convection and two-thirds radiant, although the fraction depends strongly on the temperature of interior surfaces. The cooler these surfaces, the greater the radiant fraction becomes." Hydronic systems can also go into walls and ceilings, and there are electric radiant units that mount to the wall or to the ceiling. People disagree about the degree of radiant vs. convective heating coming from walls. Radiant ceilings emit 90 percent to 95 percent of their energy as radiant heat. Both hydronic and electric radiant systems work well, and both operate quietly while minimizing the drafts and the temperature stratification that make wet, naked people uncomfortable in the bathroom.

Both types of radiant-heating systems tend to reduce energy consumption, too. Savings depend on the site conditions and the heating system used, but an often-quoted conservative figure for energy savings from radiant systems is around 20 percent compared with electric forced air, while other measures can bump the savings even higher. Figures vary from source to source, but you might be able to keep the temperature set as much as 8°F cooler than you would with forced-air or baseboard heaters and still feel the same level of comfort, thus the energy and money savings. According to Siegenthaler, "Energy savings is the icing on the cake. The cake itself is superior comfort."

# Warm Floors Are Hot Sellers

Everyone wants radiant floors. With radiant floors, you won't end up huddling near a radiator because the entire floor is the radiator. The Radiant Panel Association reports that sales of hydronic tubing for radiant heat doubled to nearly 139 million ft. between 1996 and 1999. Electric floor-warming systems are appearing rapidly, too. Some systems produce just enough heat to warm a floor and keep your feet comfortable, while others generate enough heat to warm the entire room.

## Hydronic Floor Systems, Wet and Dry

Hydronic systems circulate hot water through plastic tubes that are either embedded in a concrete slab or affixed to a plywood subfloor. If the tubes are on top of the subfloor, they run between sleepers that support the finish flooring over them. Installations requiring a poured slab are called wet applications, while stapling tubes to the subfloor is referred to as dry because there is no concrete pour. A slab of concrete can take an hour or two to heat up. For bathrooms, where the need for heat is only periodic, a system that reacts more quickly than a slab installation might be a better choice, either a thinner concrete or gypsum-concrete slab or a dry hydronic system using aluminum plates and no concrete or gypsum at all.

Laying hardwood floors over a slab can sometimes present moisture problems, so forgoing the thermal mass of a slab in favor of a dry installation may be an easier option. Dry radiant floors are light enough that they do not stress floor joists, and they allow relatively easy access to tubing in case repairs become necessary.

When poured slabs are planned anyway, running hydronic tubes in them is cost efficient—as little as $3 per sq. ft. installed. In renovations, though, if the subfloor is accessible from below, attaching radiant heating beneath the subfloor makes the most sense because it does not raise the height of the finish floor.

## Panelized Systems Offer Faster Installation

A newer, proprietary dry-hydronic configuration is Easy Floor by Modular Radiant Technologies. Easy Floor is meant as an alternative to concrete or gypsum pours. Easy Floor consists of a polypropylene grid that holds ½-in. to ⅞-in. hydronic tubes in place and conducts heat to the finish floor through a tile substrate that the company calls a Bio-Coverstone. Modular Radiant Technologies reports that it is developing cover stones that can serve as the finish floor. Like other dry-hydronic installations, Easy Floor is light enough to be installed on second and third floors. The system comes in two thicknesses, 1½ in. and 1⅛ in. Currently, the Easy Floor system is not cost efficient for projects smaller than 500–700 sq. ft., and there are thinner floor systems that can help you to avoid raising toilet flanges and making similar adjustments during a retrofit. So Easy Floor would not make sense for a single bathroom project, but as part of a larger addition or new construction, Easy Floor merits consideration.

At least three manufacturers sell prefabricated panels for hydronic-heating installations. Plasco Manufacturing Ltd. makes ThermalBoard, a ⅝-in. panel of medium-density fiberboard (MDF) with a rounded groove to capture ⅜-in. PEX tubing. To conduct heat to the subfloor, Plasco coats the entire surface with a 3-mil layer of aluminum instead of using a series of plates. ThermalBoard's list price is $4.50–$5.00 per sq. ft., plus tubing and installation.

Stadler-Viega™ offers a similar product. Its Climate Panel® is made of ½-in. plywood, uses ⁷⁄₁₆-in. O.D. tubing and affixes aluminum plates beneath the panel rather than against the subfloor, thus reflecting the heat back through the plywood. Stadler-Viega's panels are 48 in. long, coming in either 7-in. or 10-in. widths. They cost about $3.50 per sq. ft., plus tubing and installation. To attach tile floor over these panels, use cement backer board and then thinset. Attaching wood flooring requires no extra substrate, resulting in a finish floor being raised only ½ in. to ⅝ in. Laying the panels perpendicular to the flooring allows you to see the tubes as you nail. A third manufacturer, Warmboard® Inc., makes a panelized system that acts as a structural subfloor instead of adding a separate layer.

# Electric Radiant-Floor Systems Can Solve the Boiler Problem

If the house has no hydronic system, electric radiant floors are easy to install and more cost effective than installing a boiler to heat a bathroom. And electric floors raise the floor as little as ½ in. (top photo, p. 150).

Among electric radiant-floor systems, some use a single continuous wire to deliver heat, crisscrossing the floor like hydronic tubing, while others use a series of electric channels. Either way, electrical cables warm the floor controlled by an embedded temperature sensor tied back to the thermostat.

EasyHeat® says that the continuous cable system in its Warm Tiles® system "is supplied in one piece to eliminate all electrical connections in the floor," although a sensor in the floor does connect to a wall-mounted 16-amp thermostat. The cables are color-coded to indicate different amperages that can be mixed to achieve different heat outputs and to eliminate confusion during installation. This system does what the name implies—warms the tiles and not the whole space. In a reasonably warm room with no draft, a heated floor may be all you need to feel comfortable.

Bask Inc. encloses its SunTouch system's electric cable in a mesh that is simply unrolled and then embedded in the mortar beneath tile or stone floors. This sort of installation usually raises the floor only about ½ in., making it useful in retrofitting existing

## Hydronic Systems

With the growing market in hydronic radiant heating, manufacturers are working on ways to make installation faster. The panelized systems below all secure the tubing and support the finish floor. Stadler-Viega and Plasco support any type of finish flooring, while Modular Radiant Technologies markets a plastic-grid system that supports any flooring except nailed hardwood.

**STADLER-VIEGA'S CLIMATE PANEL**

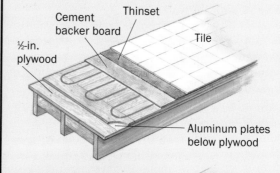

Thinset
Cement backer board
Tile
½-in. plywood
Aluminum plates below plywood

**PLASCO'S THERMALBOARD**

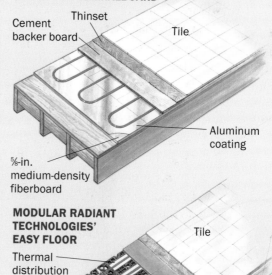

Thinset
Cement backer board
Tile
Aluminum coating
⅝-in. medium-density fiberboard

**MODULAR RADIANT TECHNOLOGIES' EASY FLOOR**

Tile
Thermal distribution plates
Thinset
Reflecting foil
Bio-Coverstone tile
Polypropylene grid

bathrooms. But at $15–$20 per sq. ft., this model is pricey.

Taking a different approach, CaloriQue's Warm Floors system uses a series of parallel resistors made of carbon and metal compounds applied to a sheet of polyester. The parallel resistors are joined at the edge by a copper-wire bus bar, and then the whole system is laminated with another layer of polyester. One advantage of this system is that anyone driving a nail through one of the resistors does not disable the whole floor, as would happen in a single-wire system. Instead, just the one resistor is interrupted, and those around it continue to function. Instead of being embedded in the subfloor, these units are stapled to the floor joists, 2 in. below the subfloor, so they will work under wood flooring as well as tile. The system comes presized for 12-in., 16-in., and 24-in. joist spacing, and is competitively priced. CaloriQue also has installation directions for systems in ceilings.

No matter what radiant-floor system you choose, there are some tips to keep in mind. Tom and Lane Meehan, who sell and install tile in Harwich, Massachusetts, were recently called out to fix a floor that someone else had installed and in which the tile was separating from the subfloor. Tom suspected that the cause of the failure was not the installation but that the owners had turned on the heat too soon, thus heating the thinset concrete before it had a chance to cure. Tom suggests waiting at least two weeks before turning on the heat in a radiant floor.

Also, Tom says that it is easy to damage coils when you're installing the tile over the electric mats. He recommends covering them with a sheet of vinyl or a piece of cardboard to protect the coils as you work back out of the bathroom. Finally, some companies offer custom-size mats. Custom mat sizes add unnecessary expense; just use standard units to warm the area you're likely to stand on.

# Radiant Walls

With all the hype that radiant floors are getting, it is easy to forget that radiant walls are another—sometimes better—option, considering both price and performance. John Siegenthaler points out that enough of the floor is covered up in some bathroom designs that even if you wanted to install one, a radiant floor alone might not generate sufficient Btus. In this case, radiant walls and ceilings are good supplements, especially ceilings over the tub area, so that bathers are warm above the water and won't have to sink down in the tub to keep from shivering. Radiant walls and ceilings can be either hydronic or electric, just like floors.

At $4–$5 per sq. ft. installed, hydronic walls are often less expensive than hydronic floors. Walls can be warmer than floors, in the 90°F to 95°F range, because people are not in constant, direct contact with walls. Wall temperatures can go even higher if need be during those subzero days if your bathroom sits against exterior walls and you need to boost output up to 60 Btu/h per sq. ft. And the response time of drywall is about 15 minutes instead of the 30 minutes to 90 minutes of floor systems.

**Radiant wall panels such as this one are available in hydronic and electric models, and vary from simple towel warmers to powerful space heaters.**

## Are Towel Warmers Another Way to Heat a Bathroom?

Towel warmers may be one way to heat a bathroom. But they're mostly to be used for supplemental heat or just plain luxury. Towel warmers can be hydronic or electric. Electric towel warmers can be hard-wired or simple plug-in models. Generally, hydronic systems provide more Btus per square foot than the electric panels do. Either one will work just to heat towels, though.

There are some inexpensive electric models on the market. Warmrails® Inc.'s towel warmers are meant to heat just towels. They use about as much power as a light bulb and range in price from $105 self-installed (40w plug-in model) to $130 plus installation (80w hard-wired model). Mostly, though, heated towel bars are an upscale item, with Myson's line ranging from $500 to $7,000.

Sometimes a towel warmer is just a towel warmer, but sometimes it's more. Some are designed to heat a room. Runtal® and Walney both market bathroom radiators that can be towel warmers, but that put out considerable heat. Runtal's 120v electric Omnipanel®, projecting 3¾ in. from the wall, is 24 in. wide by 34¾ in. tall. When set on high, it operates at 700w and generates 2400 Btu/h. Walney makes 600w electric models that should generate about 2000 Btu/h.

**Function or fashion?** This gold-plated towel warmer by Myson puts out 1350 Btu/h and costs more than $3,000.

Runtal's largest hydronic panel, which is 36 in. wide and 61 in. tall, generates about 7900 Btu/h when run with a water temperature of 180°F. Walney offers a hydronic model that generates a similar Btu figure for between $772 and $1,790, while Myson's 5200-Btu/h model costs between $1,777 and $4,822.

A typical hydronic wall starts with insulation between the studs (sources disagree about whether insulation should be faced or unfaced). Then ¾-in. furring strips are attached, leaving grooves to receive the tubing and the saddle of heat-transfer plates. On top of this layer goes ½-in. drywall.

Prefabricated panels such as Plasco's and Stadler-Viega's make installing hydronic walls fast and easy. In wall installations, radiant tubing should be installed no more than 48 in. high to avoid punctures when you're hanging pictures. Heating doesn't need to be installed behind vanities or cabinets, but special care should be taken when affixing tissue holders or anything else where hydronic wall heating is in place. To be on the safe side, take photos before you cover the panels with the drywall.

A number of manufacturers offer wall-mounted radiant panels, either hydronic or electric. Some of these panels are only

# Electric Radiant Heaters Are Unobtrusive

Electric floor warmers, such as this one manufactured by Bask, install easily. They use about as much energy as several light bulbs and raise the floor about ½ in.

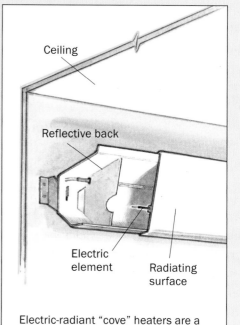

Ceiling

Reflective back

Electric element

Radiating surface

Electric-radiant "cove" heaters are a wall-mounted option. This example by Marley® Electric Heating supplements heat without taking up wall space or interfering with ceiling fixtures.

Electric radiant ceiling panels offer energy-efficient heat quickly. They also virtually disappear into the ceiling. SSHC offers one with a light, night-light, and ventilation fan built in.

towel warmers, a luxury that feels great but that doesn't radiate much extra heat. On the other hand, Runtal makes a surface-mounted radiant panel that can generate nearly 8000 Btu/h, enough to heat 200 sq. ft. Surface temperatures can be controlled by adjusting water temperature in the hydronic units.

Marley Electric Heating sells electric radiant "cove" heaters under the brand name Qmark®. Cove heaters mount on the wall a few inches from the ceiling, pulling 2.5 amps to 4.4 amps and radiating 2000–3600 Btu/h, depending on the model. A unit such as this one can provide good supplemental heat without taking up wall space or interfering with the ceiling lights.

Manufacturers of radiant ceiling heaters combat the notion that hot air rises. Infrared radiant panels heat surfaces and people directly with radiant energy, rather than heating air. Richard Watson of Solid State Heating Company (SSHC) says that SSHC's ceiling-mounted Enerjoy Radiant People-heater panels will warm a floor in about a half-hour, while more immediate heat comes off the unit, too. Each room is its own zone with this type of system, so the comfort and energy savings of custom-zone systems are easy to control. SSHC's heaters have been tested by the Department of Energy (www.doe.gov) and the National Association of Home Builders Research Center (www.nahbrc.org), and their positive reports can be read at their Web sites. SSHC's panels can be surface-mounted, protrude about an inch, and respond quickly due to their low mass. Similar panels are made by Qmark, which distributes through contractors and supply houses.

Depending on your current wiring, you could install an electric radiant-ceiling panel rated at up to 1640w using the existing wiring from your overhead light, and be done in one day. No tearing up the floor, no rewiring, no mess. SSHC's Bathroom Comfort Center units combine a radiant panel with a light, night-light, and exhaust fan, and sell for $350–$500, depending on size.

# Which Heat Source Should You Pick?

If I were building new, I'd consider hydronic floors and walls or radiant ceiling heat. In retrofits, radiant floors and walls are still possible but might be costly. If I were otherwise happy with my bathroom but wanted a little extra heat, I'd look at electric units.

Think also about using more than one heat source, either for convenience or for extra comfort. For instance, what about an electric floor warmer for comfort, a hydronic baseboard for primary heat, and a towel warmer that you will love every time you use it?

* Price estimates noted are from 2002.

**David Ericson** is an assistant editor at Fine Homebuilding.

---

## Sources

**Bask SunTouch**
3131 W. Chestnut Expressway
Springfield, MO 65802
(888) 432-8932
www.suntouch.net

**Calorique**
2380 Cranberry Hwy.
West Wareham, MA 02576
(508) 291-4224
www.calorique.com

**Easyheat**
2 Connecticut South Dr.
East Granby, CT 06026
(800) 523-7636
www.easyheat.com

**Marley Electric Heating**
c/o Marley Engineered Products
470 Beauty Spot Rd.
Bennettsville, SC 29512
(800) 452-4179
www.mearleymeh.com

**Modular Radiant Technologies**
P.O. Box 2067
Vashon, WA 98070
(206) 463-1267
www.pfg-industries.com

**Myson Inc.**
948 Hercules Dr., Suite 4
Colchester, VT 05446
(800) 698-9690
www.mysoninc.com

**Nutone**
4820 Redbank Rd.
Cincinnati, OH 45227
(888) 336-6155
www.nutone.com

**Plasco Manufacturing**
655 Park St.
Regina, Saskatchewan
S4N 5N1
Canada
(800) 752-7260

**The Radiant Panel Association**
P.O. Box 717
Loveland, CO 80539
(800) 660-7187
www.rpa-info.com

**Runtal North America, Inc.**
187 Neck Rd.
P.O. Box 8278
Ward Hill, MA 01835
(800) 526-2621
www.runtalnorth-america.com

**Slant/Fin**
100 Forest Dr.
Greenvale, NY 11548
(800) 775-4552
www.slantfin.com

**SSHC, Inc.**
P.O. Box 769
Old Saybrook, NY 06475
(800) 544-5182
www.sshcinc.com

**Stadler-Viega**
3 Alfred Cir.
Bedford, MA 01730
(718) 275-3122
www.stadlercorp.com

**VRV Products**
1875 Dewey Ave.
Benton Harbor, MI 49022
(616) 925-8818
www.vrvproducts.com

**Walney**
404 Elm Ave.
North Wales, PA 19454
(800) 650-1484
www.walney-online.com

**Warmboard**
9498 SW Barbur Blvd., #203
Portland, OR 97219
(503) 977-1011
www.warmboard.com

**Warmrails**
2930 Grace Lane, Suite H
Costa Mesa, CA 92626
(714) 957-4317
www.warmrails.com

# CREDITS

The articles compiled in this book appeared in the following issues of *Fine Homebuilding*:

p. iii: Photo © Randi Baird.

Table of contents: Photos on p. iv (left) © Karen Melvin (design by Eric Oder and Ollie Foran, SALA Architects); p. iv (right) by Scott Phillips, © The Taunton Press, Inc.; p. 1 (left) by Roe A. Osborn, courtesy *Fine Homebuilding,* © The Taunton Press, Inc.; and p. 1 (right) © Claudio Santini (design by Steven and Cathi House).

p. 4: Ten Important Elements of a Good Bathroom by David Edrington, issue 127. Photos by Charles Miller, courtesy *Fine Homebuilding,* © The Taunton Press, Inc. Illustrations by Vince Babak, © The Taunton Press, Inc.

p. 12: Accessible Bathrooms by Margaret Wylde, Adrian Baron-Robbins, and Sam Clark, issue 88. Photos on p. 16 (top left) courtesy Aqua Glass®; p. 16 (top right and bottom right) courtesy HEWI®; and p. 16 (bottom left) Med/West. Illustrations by Vince Babak, © The Taunton Press, Inc.

p. 19: A Gallery of Favorite Bath Details by Charles Bickford, issue 143. Photos on pp. 19 (left) and 24 © Randi Baird; pp. 19 (center), and 21 (top) by Kevin Ireton, courtesy *Fine Homebuilding,* © The Taunton Press, Inc.; pp. 19 (right) and 25 (bottom) © Karen Melvin; pp. 20 (left), 21 (bottom), and 23 (bottom) by Charles Bickford, courtesy *Fine Homebuilding,* © The Taunton Press, Inc.; p. 20 (right) © Brian Vanden Brink; p. 22 © Ken Gutmaker; p. 23 (top) © Ken Peterson; and p. 25 (top) © Peter Judge (design by Berle Pilsk.)

p. 26: Choosing a Toilet by Steve Culpepper, issue 112. Photos on pp. 27 and 32 (top) courtesy Toto; p. 32 (center and bottom) courtesy Kohler; p. 33 (top) courtesy Incinolet; p. 33 (center) courtesy Advanced Composting Systems; p. 33 (bottom) courtesy BioLet; p. 34 (top) courtesy Eljer; p. 34 (center) courtesy American Standard; and p. 34 (bottom) courtesy Burgess

International. Illustration by Bob La Pointe, © The Taunton Press, Inc.

p. 36: How to Install a Toilet by Peter Hemp, issue 121. Photos by Charles Miller, courtesy *Fine Homebuilding,* © The Taunton Press, Inc. Illustration by Dan Thornton, © The Taunton Press, Inc.

p. 44: Plastic Tub-Showers by Scott Gibson, issue 119. Photos by Scott Gibson, courtesy *Fine Homebuilding,* © The Taunton Press, Inc.

p. 54: Installing a Leakproof Shower Pan by Tom Meehan, issue 141. Photos by Roe A. Osborn, courtesy *Fine Homebuilding,* © The Taunton Press, Inc. Illustration by Rick Daskam, © The Taunton Press, Inc.

p. 62: A Walk Through Shower Doors by Andy Engel, issue 135. Photos on p. 63 © Claudio Santini (bathroom design: House + House Architects); p. 64 courtesy Kohler; pp. 65, 66 (bottom), 69, and 70 by Andy Engel, courtesy *Fine Homebuilding,* © The Taunton Press, Inc.; and p. 66 (top) courtesy Basco.

p. 72: Residential Steam Showers by Andy Engel issue 143. Photos on pp. 73 (top) and 75 by Roe A. Osborn, courtesy *Fine Homebuilding,* © The Taunton Press, Inc.; p. 73 (bottom) © Dean Dellaventura; p. 74 (top) by Andy Engel, courtesy *Fine Homebuilding,* © The Taunton Press, Inc.; p. 74 (bottom) courtesy Kohler; and p. 76 courtesy Sussman Lifestyle Corp.

p. 77: Choosing a Lavatory Faucet by Andrew Wormer, issue 113. Photos on p. 77 by Charles Miller, courtesy *Fine Homebuilding,* © The Taunton Press, Inc.; and pp. 78–87 by Scott Phillips, courtesy *Fine Homebuilding,* © The Taunton Press, Inc. Illustrations by Bob La Pointe, © The Taunton Press, Inc.

p. 86: Tiling a Bathroom Floor by Dennis Hourany, issue 124. Photos by Scott Gibson, courtesy *Fine Homebuilding,* © The Taunton Press, Inc. Illustration by Dan Thornton, © The Taunton Press, Inc.

p. 97: Tiling a Tub Surround by Michael Byrne, issue 92. Photos by Kevin Ireton, courtesy *Fine Homebuilding,* © The Taunton Press, Inc.

p. 106: Tiling a Shower with Marble by Tom Meehan, issue 98. Photos by Jefferson Kolle, courtesy *Fine Homebuilding,* © The Taunton Press, Inc.

p. 113: Tiling with Limestone by Tom Meehan, issue 118. Photos by Roe A. Osborn, courtesy *Fine Homebuilding,* © The Taunton Press, Inc.

p. 123: Silicone Caulking Basics by Brian Zavitz, issue 111. Photos on p. 123 by Scott Phillips, courtesy *Fine Homebuilding,* © The Taunton Press, Inc.; and pp. 124–127 by Steve Culpepper, courtesy *Fine Homebuilding,* © The Taunton Press, Inc.

p. 128: A Look at Bathroom Lighting by Andrew Wormer, issue 127. Photos on p. 129 © Christopher Irion (design by architect Philip Mathews); p. 131 © Claudio Santini (design by Steven and Cathi House); p. 133 © Grey Crawford; and p. 134 by Kevin Ireton, courtesy *Fine Homebuilding,* © The Taunton Press, Inc. Illustrations by Paul Perreault, © The Taunton Press, Inc.

p. 136: Choosing and Installing a Bathroom-Vent Fan by Rex Cauldwell, issue 115. Photos on pp. 137, 139, and 141 © Susan Kahn; and p. 138 by Roe A. Osborn, courtesy *Fine Homebuilding,* © The Taunton Press, Inc. Illustrations by Mark Hannon, © The Taunton Press, Inc.

p. 142: What's Hot in Bathroom Heaters? by David Ericson, issue 135. Photos on p. 144 (#1–4) courtesy NuTone; p. 144 (#5) courtesy VRV Products; p. 148 courtesy Runtal; p. 149 courtesy Myson; p. 150 (top) courtesy Bask; and p. 150 (bottom) courtesy SSHC. Illustrations by Rick Daskam, © The Taunton Press, Inc.

# INDEX

## A

Accessibility, 12–18
  doors and, 13
  faucet, 15, 17
  handholds and, 13–14, 15, 16
  handicap/wheelchair, 13–18
  nonslip surfaces and, 18
  public vs. private, 12
  shower/tub, 15, 16
  sink/countertop, 15–17
  toilet, 13, 14–15, 16
Accessories, 11

## B

Backer board:
  adhesives, 91
  expansion gaps, 90
  to floor spacing, 60, 107
  limestone tile, 115–16
  marble tile, 107–108
  shower wall, 60
  taping, 93, 94, 99
  tile floor, 88, 90, 93, 94
  tub surround, 98–99
Backsplashes, continuous, 21
Ball valves, 84, 86
Bathing, 11
Bathtubs. *See* Tubs; Tub-showers
Bullnose tiles, 102–103, 110

## C

Cartridge valves, 83–84
Caulking:
  shower doors, 65
  silicone, 123–27
  toilets, 43
Ceiling dimensions, 9
Ceramic-disk valves, 81, 84–85
Ceramic tile. *See* Tile flooring; Tile tub surrounds
Clearances, fixture, 9, 13, 17
Compression valves, 81–83
Control lines, 88, 91–92
Countertops
  accessibility of, 15–17
  continuous backsplashes and, 21

## D

Dimensions:
  fixture, 9, 13
  horizontal/vertical, 9
Doors, 13
Drain pipes, 30, 37–38

## E

Electric floor heating, 145, 147–48, 150, 151
Entrance transitions, 4
Exhaust fans, 11, 18, 136–41
  air volume of, 136–37
  combination, 128, 137–39, 144
  installing, 139–41
  quiet, 133, 137

  sources for, 11, 141
  venting, 138
  wiring, 139–41

## F

Faucets, 77–87
  accessibility of, 17
  brass, 78–80
  composition of, 78–80
  flow control of, 87
  good-quality, 10–11
  handle types of, 80–81
  lever-controlled, 80–81
  one- vs. two-handle, 80
  Physical vapor deposition (PVD), 79–80
  selection of, 17, 85–87
  sources for, 11
  stem vs. wide-spread, 80
  valve types in, 81–85, 86
Fixtures
  clearances/heights of, 9, 13, 17
  functionality of, 10–11
  sources for, 11, 18
  *See also individual fixtures*
Floor heaters. *See* Heaters
Flooring:
  limestone tile, 113–22
  marble tile, 110–11
  materials, 10
  nonslip, 18
  radiant-heated, 145–48, 150–51
  wood, 10
  *See also* Tile flooring

## G

Grout:
  floor, 95–96
  limestone tile, 120–22
  marble tile, 112
  mixing, 95
  for steam showers, 74
  trowels, 95, 96, 104
  tub surround, 98, 104–105

## H

Handholds, 13–14, 15, 16
Handicap access. *See* Accessibility
Heaters, 142–51
  accessibility of, 18
  electric floor, 145, 147–48, 150, 151
  exhaust fans with, 137–39, 144
  hydronic floor, 145, 146–47, 150, 151
  radiant, 145–51
  sizing rules for, 143
  sources for, 151
  stand-alone, 143–45
  towel warmers as, 149
  wall, 148–51
Heights, fixture, 9
Horizontal dimensions, 9
Hydronic floor heating, 145, 145–47, 150, 151

## L

Lavatories. *See* Sinks
Lighting, 128–35
  accent, 130
  accessibility of, 18
  ambient, 25
  bathing and, 11
  color/cost specs, 132
  decorative, 130, 134–35
  exhaust fans with, 128, 137–39
  fixtures vs. lamps, 135
  general, 130, 133–34
  glossary, 130
  goal of, 130
  hidden, 25
  Hollywood, 131
  lamp types, 132, 135
  natural, 6, 8, 17, 130, 132
  recessed, 128, 134
  rope, 134, 135
  sconce, 9
  sources for, 135
  task, 130
  tub/shower, 9, 18, 130, 132–33
  vanity, 128–32
  vertical, 130–31
  windows and, 6, 8, 23
Limestone tile, 113–22
  backer board, 115–16
  colors/origins, 115
  cutting/shaping, 115–17
  grouting, 120–22
  layout, 113–15
  marble tile vs., 115
  mural installation, 118–19
  scratch repair, 120
  sealing, 120–22
  shower niches, 121
  sorting, 113–15
  sources for, 122
  steam showers and, 74
  thinset, 74, 115–16
  waterproofing membrane and, 121
Linoleum, 10

## M

Marble tile, 106–12
  backer-board installation, 107–108
  blending colors of, 106–107
  borders, 110
  bullnosing, 110
  cleaning, 112
  floors, 110–11
  grouting, 112
  installing, 108–12
  limestone tile vs., 115
  sealing, 108–109
  showers, 106–12
  sources for, 112
  steam showers and, 74
  thinset, 109, 111
  trowels for, 108, 109, 111
Medicine cabinets, 11, 23
Mirrors:
  accessibility of, 18
  lighting and, 128–32
Mold and mildew, 136
Mortar. *See* Thinset
Murals, limestone, 118–19

## P

Paint, water-resistant, 10
Physical vapor deposition (PVD), 79–80
Privacy, 6, 12, 13
Proportions, roomlike, 4, 5–6, 7
Public accessibility, 12
PVD. *See* Physical vapor deposition

## R

Radiant heating, 145–51

## S

Sconces, 9
Sealing tile, 74, 108–109, 120–22
Shower doors, 62–71
  caulking, 65, 123–27
  clear-plastic seals for, 71
  frameless, 68, 69–70, 71
  glass, 65–66, 68
  hinged screen, 66–67
  hinges for, 69–70
  installation checklist for, 67
  sliding, 62–65, 66
  sources for, 71
  stationary panel, 70–71
  steam, 73, 74
  tracks for, 62–65
Shower pans, 54–61
  backer-board installation for, 60
  drain connection for, 59
  floor pitch of, 55–57
  mud layer of, 60–61
  schematic of, 55
  sources for, 61
  testing, 54, 59–60
  vinyl membrane of, 57–60
Showers:
  accessibility of, 15, 16
  built-in niches for, 121
  dimensions of, 9
  lighting for, 130, 132–33
  marble tile, 106–12
  seats in, 16, 111
  sources for, 18
  views from, 7, 9
  wall materials for, 10
  windows and, 6, 8, 23
  without boundaries, 20, 22
  *See also* Steam showers; Tile tub surrounds; Tub-
    showers
Silicone caulk, 123–27
  advantages/disadvantages, 123–24
  bead size, 125–26
  color selection, 124–25
  materials/tools for, 124–25, 126–27
  preparation for, 125
  storing, 127
Sinks:
  accessibility of, 15–17
  custom, 20
  dimensions of, 9
  *See also* Vanities
Soap holder height, 9
Sources, 11, 18
  exhaust fan, 11, 141
  heater, 151
  lighting, 135
  limestone tile, 122
  marble tile, 112

shower door, 71
shower pan, 61
steam shower, 75
tile supply, 96, 105
toilet, 35
tub-shower, 18, 53
Space:
    accessibility and, 13
    fixtures and, 9, 13, 17
    horizontal/vertical, 9
    intimate, 6
    proportions, 5–6, 7
    transitions and, 4
Steam showers, 72–76
    doors for, 73, 74
    enclosures for, 72–74
    grouting, 74
    hardware placement in, 76
    sources for, 75
    steam generators for, 75–76
    tiling advice for, 74
    unique requirements of, 72–75
Switch-plate covers, 11

**T**

Thinset:
    limestone tile, 115–16
    marble tile, 109, 111
    tile floor, 92–94
    tub surround, 99, 100–103
Tile, uses of, 10
Tile flooring, 88–96
    backer-board installation, 88, 90, 93, 94
    cutting tiles for, 91–92
    grouting, 95–96
    layout/control lines, 88, 91–92
    radiant heat and, 147
    resetting tile in, 95
    sources for, 96
    subfloor preparation, 89–90
    thinset, 92–94
    trowels for, 93, 94, 95, 96
    See also Limestone tile; Marble tile
Tile tub surrounds, 97–105
    backer-board installation for, 98–99
    cutting/drilling tiles for, 103
    field tiles for, 101–102
    framing and waterproofing, 98
    grouting, 97, 104–105
    layout of, 100
    sources for, 105
    steam shower, 74
    thinset for, 99, 100–103
    trim tiles for, 99, 102–103
    trowels for, 101
Toilet-paper holder height, 9
Toilets, 26–35, 36–43
    accessibility of, 13, 16
    anchoring, 38, 39, 40–41
    caulking, 43
    color/shape of, 35
    composting/incinerating, 33
    defects in, 40
    dimensions/spacing of, 9, 13
    drain pipes for, 30, 37–38
    flanges for, 38–40
    flush capacity of, 26–28, 30
    framing for, 37
    manufacturing process of, 30

mechanics of, 28–29
    1.6-gal. gravity, 26–30, 31
    plunging, 29
    power-assist, 31
    schematic of, 28
    setting, 40–42
    sources for, 35
    special, 32–34
    tank installation in, 41–42
    wall-mounted, 16
    water supply of, 9, 42–43
    wax rings for, 38–40
Toothbrush holder height, 9
Towel bars, 11
    heights of, 9
    on windowsill, 24
Towel warmers, 149
Trowels
    grout, 95, 96, 104
    marble tile, 108, 109, 111
    margin, 94
    tile floor, 93, 94, 95, 96
    wall tile, 101
Tubs:
    accessibility of, 14, 15
    dimensions of, 9
    enameled cast-iron, 10
    lighting for, 130, 132–33
    sources for, 18
    See also Tile tub surrounds
Tub-showers, 44–53
    acrylic, 44–46, 50–51, 53
    advantages of, 44–46, 48–49
    ANSI standards for, 51–53
    certified, 51–53
    choosing, 53
    Gelcoat/fiberglass, 44–47, 48–49, 53
    installation tips for, 52
    lighting for, 130, 132–33
    manufacturing process of, 46–47, 48–49, 50–51
    multi-piece, 47, 48–49, 50
    sources for, 53
    See also Tile tub surrounds

**V**

Valves, 81–85
    ball, 84, 86
    cartridge, 83–84
    ceramic-disk, 81, 84–85
    compression, 81–83
Vanities:
    accessibility of, 17
    custom, 21
    lighting for, 128–32
Vent fans. See Exhaust fans
Vertical dimensions, 9
Views, borrowed, 7, 9
Vinyl flooring, 10

**W**

Wall coverings, effect of, 9
Water-resistant finishes, 9, 10
Wheelchair access. See Accessibility
Windows, 6, 8, 23
Wood floors, 10